Earthrise

Earthrise

Queer novels and the lives of
LGBTQ persons

by

Dwight Cathcart

Adriana Books
Boston, Massachusetts
2019

Adriana Books
Adrianabooks.com
Boston, Massachusetts

Front cover photograph: Earthrise, NASA

The Earthrise essays were originally published as posts to the blog on my website Adriana Books. *adrianabooks.com.* The date of original publication is given below the text on the last page of each essay.

Printed from:
earthrise text 20200216
earthrise cover 20200216

Earthrise

Preface

It is a truth that LGBTQ persons do not have a literature that reflects us. We have a literature that reflects some of us, and we have a literature that reflects many of us partially. We don't have a literature that reflects how varied the community is and how different we can be, one from another. How differently we are treated and how differently we respond to our treatment. We differ by race, class, geography, gender and age, among other qualities. Our literature largely ignores our political predicament—that our "rights" are limited and depend on one vote in the Supreme Court. We don't have novels about LGBTQ people who are discriminated against and abused and murdered. Channing Smith killed himself September 23, 2019 because he had been bullied and his notes to his friend were made public. He was sixteen years old. We have few adult novels about gay teen-aged suicides. The thinness of our literature is mainly a result of the wholesale purchase of the publishing industry by large media corporations, the large distributors, large booksellers who deal in the economies of scale, and writers who hesitate to write about the real lives of LGBTQ because they don't think we are interested or are afraid. But we are interested, and some of us are not afraid. We know we are being abused, yet our literature doesn't show characters who rebel. We ought to be asking about our literature, *Does this book in any serious way reflect our lives?* Usually it doesn't, and these *Earthrise* essays look at the effect of that failure.

Earthrise 1

The picture on the cover of this little book was taken December 24, 1968, while three astronauts from NASA's Apollo 8 program were circling the moon. Bill Anders took the picture, and the other two astronauts on the craft with him were Frank Borman and Jim Lovell. The picture was the first photograph to show the Earth's spherical shape. This year, it will have been fifty years since the picture was taken. The picture is called "Earthrise." There have been two other images of the universe, each of which has had a long life. One is the Ptolemaic image, from the writings of Claudius Ptolemy in the second century CE, in which the Earth is drawn in the center of a sheet of paper, surrounded by the various planets which move around the Earth in what some called "crystalline spheres." Drawings, engravings, and woodcuts of this conception were ubiquitous throughout the Middle Ages, and most people would have been familiar with it. The message the image sent to viewers was *this is where we are in the universe,* at the center, with its accompanying belief, *our lives matter.*

It wasn't to last. A second image began to appear in the sixteenth century. *The Sun was at the center.* This conception of the universe was the result of the work of the astronomer Nicolaus Copernicus. During Shakespeare's time, this image— the Copernican or heliocentric system—moved the Earth off to

Earthrise 1

the side, to the third planet from the Sun, a loss of celestial status disturbing for many people. John Donne wrote of this moment in the *First Anniversary: An Anatomy of the World*, "And new philosophy"—which is what he called the new science—"calls all in doubt, the element of fire is quite put out. The truth is lost, and no man knows where to look for it." *First Anniversary: An Anatomy of the World,* ll. 205-208.

Now *Earthrise*. The image taken by the astronauts in 1968 tells us that it is not just that we are not at the center of things, it is that we are very very far from the next big thing. And, even worse, our position, wherever that is, is not stable. We are "falling." This is NASA's word. Our planet is "falling" through space. Space is huge, black, mostly empty, and our home, however beautiful that blue marble, can be swallowed up in that silent blackness. We don't know what we are falling toward.

Earthrise

When *Earthrise* was first published, it embodied a worldview as powerful and freighted and as ubiquitous as a picture of a sunset—or the Ptolemaic and Copernican systems before it.What the photograph said to the men who brought it back from space was that the Earth seemed fragile, there in the blackness of space. So small. And people can see that we live very close to one another in a tiny corner of the universe. Whatever differences exist between nations and races and ethnicities and genders and sexualities are trivial compared to the vastness of space. Even the words in our languages—*big, vast, immense*—are made to be measured in miles and kilometers and are utterly worthless indicating the size of space. We appear to be alone. There is no God, no one to tell us that we are his children. No one to say, *Do this, Do that. Don't do all these other things.* This photograph meant immediately, when it came out, that we are the only adults in this room, and it led almost immediately to the Earth Movement, to Earth Day, to environmentalism and to support for ecological movements —to caring for the Earth. We have to do it, and we have to do it ourselves for ourselves. This is our only home.

The astronauts who brought back *Earthrise* made another point. Falling through space on such a tiny tiny fragile chariot ought to make it easier to work together and to help each other to survive, ought to make it easier to see the fatuous malignant stupidity of a thought like *America First.*

The Tree of Life

A trope that has become familiar to many people is the one Malick's movie *Tree of Life* presents, where the camera, which starts out with the black screen showing the white letters of the words from Job—*Where were you when I laid the foundations of the Earth?*—focusses on a suburban neighborhood near Waco, Texas, and suddenly shows, as in a flashback, the gas clouds of space and the churning cauldron of the surface of the Sun, the Big Bang and the beginning of everything. The people in that neighborhood in Waco include a man and his wife and their two sons, and it is not long before it appears that the couple's younger son has been killed in a war. The death of the son—the surviving son, whose name is Jack, is played by Sean Penn when he's older, and it is he who is remembering everything that happens in this movie—places the story of the son's death and his grieving parents solidly in the context of the story of Job.

Earthrise—remember, we used to be in the middle of everything—insists on our memory, on our remembering the other ways we used to see our place in the universe, because these successive images document our unceasing need to discover who we are and who we are becoming. It matters that we know where we are in the universe. A person can be afraid, and the process of discovering where we are and who we are can be painful. I see *Earthrise*, and I think of all the men and women who have looked up at the night sky—spent hundreds and thousands of hours looking up at the night sky—trying to figure it out, exposing their need to know, searching for meaning, putting themselves at risk of discovering that there is no meaning. And we are nobody.

But *up* is only one of the directions *Earthrise* directs us. In *Tree of Life*, from the capture of the gas clouds, the camera zooms in on Earth and gets closer and closer until almost the entire screen of the cinema is taken up by a single biological cell. Then there are two cells, they join, and life begins. *Tree of Life* insists on an immensely increased scope of our vision, from the gas clouds in a galaxy down to a biological cell, to life in the sea, then on land. This is vertigo inducing. We have seen woodcuts or engravings—which are themselves merely fantasies—of the cosmos, but now we have photographs and have the ability to move smoothly from the gas clouds to the cell, to life, each one implicit in the presence of the other. At the end of the twentieth century and now in the first decades of the twenty-first, this is now the scope of our lives. This is the way we live—with microscope and telescope, from chemical elements to living beings and then back again.

In *The Earth Gazers: On Seeing Ourselves* Christopher Potter tells us that the astronauts came back to Earth exalted. What they saw was *unspeakable*. The experience of seeing Earth from space was too awesome for them to speak of. What it was that the astronauts saw and couldn't speak of was us on our fragile, beautiful home in their camera viewfinders. The

Earthrise 1

astronauts went into space to see what was there and ended by seeing *us* and where we live. *Earthrise.*

Aside from the technical achievements of *Earthrise*—how do you get a camera to the moon?—and even aside from its effect on our philosophical understanding of ourselves, the photograph has another effect. The photographic complexity of the view of *Earthrise*—a photograph taken from the moon looking toward us—made it essential that a person be able to see outer and inner at once, the external and the internal, the infinitely large and the infinitesimally small. In one universally accessible photograph, people are invited, even compelled, to expand their vision in both directions at once. They are invited to see the similarity between things, not their differences, the linkages among people and animals and plants and trees—and the Earth. Me and you. Past and present. Simultaneously.

The contribution that *The Tree of Life* and other movies make by linking what is happening here on Earth—grief for a dead son—to the context of the immense blackness and emptiness of space expands to include at least the possibility that other kinds of links will connect us and our life on Earth to dark space. The ancient and most elemental of links—cause leading to effect, the past leading to the future—might be found not to be the most important for an understanding of our lives. We understand our lives by the fact that under our feet is the Earth. With *Earthrise,* we have photographic evidence that our lives exist in other places than Earth, where there is no physical contact between us and Earth, and that no thing gives our lives meaning but ourselves.

The arrangement of objects in *Earthrise* is disorienting—the foreground is the Moon, and the background is the Earth and space. It is a radical reorientation of the normal, but of course it is itself the true normal, and we realize that the way we have always seen it—us and our universe at the center—is in error.

The two narratives in the movie—the events going on in space leading to the human life going on in the Waco suburb—are linked in the movie by time. In Malick's beginning, there are sun spots and flares, the gas clouds in space, then a whole series of images of gas clouds, a sphere, the sun, and a volcano, leading to hot springs, and eventually to the creation of life, and what began as the grief that Mrs. O'Brien experiences is set against the creation of life on Earth.

It may be that the before-and-after arrangement of *Tree of Life* is superseded by what is implicit in *Earthrise*. We know creation is still going on while Mrs. O'Brien (Jessica Chastain) is grieving the death of her son. There is a contemporaneity about these events that alters our understanding of them. Creation is going on everywhere—the creation of stars, moons, suns, planets, black holes, dark matter, all animal and plant life —and the destruction of lives and worlds going on at the same time, everywhere. *Earthrise* is the kind of civilization-shattering event matched by only a few other events—I can think of only Darwin's *Descent of Man*, Einstein's *Theory of Relativity*, and the first performances of *Hamlet* and *King Lear* and *Oedipus* and compositions by Bach, Mozart, and surely one by John Lennon. What we are left with is the silence of Mrs. O'Brien's grief amid the silence of black space. But the universe is still expanding, and things still grow.

The tension between this destruction and this growing is the *sine qua non* of the condition of our lives and is what, I presume, has always driven men and women to sail to the Indies and fly to Paris and to go to the moon and to paint the *Guernica* and to refuse to give up her seat in a Birmingham bus. In the blackness of space, no God, no one, hears Mrs. O'Brien weep for the death of her son. What gives her weeping

Earthrise 1

meaning is that she hears herself—*my son's life is worth my weeping*—and, in Malick's movie, Jack weeps for his brother, and Mr. O'Brien for his son. Mrs. O'Brien's grief gives meaning to everything and everybody around her. People, by going to the Moon, by creating life here on Earth, by creating art—surrounded as they are by the deep indifferent silent blackness of space, as in a frame—by their work, are the only source of meaning. I made this.

April 19, 2018

Earthrise 2

Two weeks ago, on April 26, 2018, the Legacy Museum and Memorial for Peace and Justice opened in Montgomery, Alabama, funded by the Equal Justice Institute. This is the only museum and memorial in this nation dedicated to the victims of the crime of lynching. The memorial is a large building, open to the outdoors, in which steel cases or boxes hang from the ceiling, and, they say, when you enter the memorial, you are walking among these weathered steel cases. But as you proceed, the ground under you recedes slightly and you find the steel cases are hanging higher and higher above you, until the metaphor is clear. The steel cases hang above your head like the bodies of the 4400 men and women lynched in the South before 1950 and hanging from the limbs of trees in black-and-white photographs which all of us have seen. The steel boxes have the names of as many of the persons as are available. There is one box for each county in which lynchings took place.

It seems, from the pictures, to be a large memorial, but it is not large enough to be seen from space. Not as large, say, as the Great Pyramid of Cheops, which can be seen from space and which holds the mortal remains of one Pharaoh of Egypt, even though the Memorial for Peace and Justice in Montgomery memorializes 4400 men and women.

According to the published statements of the EJI and

according to comments posted on the web, the museum takes its place in the national debate over who we are. *Did we really own slaves? Did we really treat other humans like that? When did that stop? Did lynching succeed slavery or did it happen at least partially at the same time? When did lynching stop? Did it ever stop? Was the murder of Emmet Till a lynching? And should all the murders of black people in recent years by white officials really be called lynchings?*

The answers to all these questions are *yes, yes, 1863, partially at the same time, well uh…, no, yes, yes.*

If an astronaut turned his camera toward Earth, he would see the same lovely blue marble as is seen in *Earthrise,* but he wouldn't see the way we have treated each other. Neither would a traveller from deep space see how we have treated each other. Despite *Star Trek* and all the other science fiction stories there are out there, those in space are not going to know or care about our fights here on earth. What gives Mrs. O'Brien's grief meaning is that it is she who grieves, and the people around her know. *I lost my son.* And what the people of the Equal Justice Institute have done in Montgomery in the memorial is to say, *We know these men and women were murdered by angry mobs.* We know this happened. Now all the rest of you must acknowledge it too. This is what humans have done. We must remember.

This is an effect of the memory, and it raises the question, *Why must we remember?* It is not merely that we remember so we won't do it again—won't lynch men from trees or whatever the crime is—and so they can't do it to us again, but we remember because we need to know ourselves. We are the biological organisms who seek to exterminate our fellow species-members, and we are the biological organisms who are regularly extinguished by our fellow species-members. This is unanswerable. And we must remember because our memory tells us what we are capable of doing and being, and what we are capable of, we do, that is, we are murderers and the victims of murderers. We are also many other things—our species created the Mozart *Requiem,* the Belvedere *Torso,* the Taj Mahal—and if we are going to remember, and we will remember, we cannot help that because our memory is built into what we are. We are going to have to remember *David* and the men and women whose names are on those weathered steel boxes hanging from the roof of the Memorial to Peace and Justice in Montgomery, Alabama. We cannot pick and choose, remember some things but not others. We cannot choose when we will remember or what we will remember. We cannot choose to remember.

I have told my husband, that I will go anywhere with him to live as long as that place has a great library and a great museum. Libraries and museums are two depositories of memory in our culture. The repertoire of the Boston Symphony Orchestra is another. The Boston Gay Men's Chorus is also. In museums, we remember how El Greco saw saints, how Turner saw slave ships, how Sargent saw Thomas McKellar. In big museums, we remember everything. All the museums together are our collective memory. This is the way men and women saw themselves and their lives. And an individual, standing in a gallery, cannot be human and, at the same time, refuse to remember. The woman in the painting with the big gray wig, the jewelry, the long dress, and the tiny pointed shoes, is one of us. One of the points of travel and of education is to broaden one's perspective, to expand one's point of view to include different cultures, different time periods, different aspects of culture. It is an inescapable part of our personhood, that we seek to know about each other.

Dylan Jones, writing in *Attitude*, says "young queer

people shouldn't be obliged to care about LGBT history and that's the biggest sign of our political success there is." (February 7, 2018) Well, this has been said before and is said wherever and whenever LGBTQ people gather. So much has changed, such important changes have been made, that the past has nothing to do with our lives. But it is not the only thing being said. Lance Richardson, writing in *Slate*, in a piece entitled, "Family Jewels, How a box of queer artifacts from 1963 helped make sense of my gay life today," attacks the heart of the matter when he opens the box and discovers what is inside and how deeply the objects affect and reflect his own gay life fifty years later. The History Projects around the country are evidence of the wind blowing. There is, here in Boston, an archive of Gay and Lesbian History. And it is important to remember that women, people of color, and every other minority have come to a point in their progress to full-fledged American citizenship when they realize it is important to remember their history, when they started writing books, poetry, histories, novels, and making movies, or composing songs. In every minority the third wave of their progress, after civil disobedience in the streets, and after the initial legislative and judicial progress has been made, has consisted of an intense look at themselves, answering the question, *How is it for you there?* and *How did you get here?* In Boston there is a monument to Notable Women on Commonwealth Avenue and the monument to the 54th Volunteer Regiment across from the State House, and now, in Montgomery, there is the Monument to Peace and Justice. As we are human, we cannot stop remembering. The LGBTQ communities have not yet reached this point.

The central event in LGBTQ literature is a person's coming out. We get that over and over, and that would be OK if a person lived in a culture which was perfectly OK with gay people and where gay people have never been abused by persons in authority. But we don't live in a culture like that. Even though we have marriage equality, the press regularly abuses gay people, and we read reports on anti-gay murders and physical and emotional abuse. Abuse of gay people has not ended with the arrival of marriage equality, and that means that LGBTQ people have much to acknowledge from the past and from the present.

One of the principal modes of memory is the written word. Poems. Novels. Histories. Plays. But in our community—the LGBTQ community—we don't seem to be much interested in exploring ourselves or, even less, our past. Ten years or so ago, people in the publishing industry said that the market for gay books had *vanished.* Then, a little later, I was told by a friend in the UK that the market for gay books had *collapsed.* Gay bookstores across the country have closed. Boston doesn't have even one any more. Gay bars close. People continue to read— beach reading largely, beautiful boys falling in love with beautiful boys, and the novels by writers who established themselves before the collapse—but we don't read on the order of the Monument to Peace and Justice. Big, comprehensive, honest. Look at our recent major movies. *Brokeback Mountain, Moonlight, Call Me by Your Name.* All about coming out. Nothing that tells us who we have been and how we got here. What we are to do. We don't seem interested.

This is about life on Earth as we live it on a planet in space. *How should we live? What should we do?* I think we should visit the Memorial for Peace and Justice and learn about lynching, but we should also learn about the past, learn what we have done, learn what has been done to us, learn our place in the universe.

May 11, 2018

13

Earthrise 3

This, said to us by the man who says of himself, "Call me Ishmael:"

It [the spermiceti] had cooled and crystallized to such a degree, that when, with several others, I sat down before a large Constantine's bath of it, I found it strangely concreted into lumps, here and there, rolling about in the liquid part. It was our business to squeeze these lumps back into fluid. A sweet and unctious duty! No wonder that in old times this sperm was such a favorite cosmetic. Such a clearer! such a sweetener! such a softener! such a delicious mollifier! After having my hands in it for only a few minutes, my fingers felt like eels, and began, as it were, to serpentine and spiralize. As I sat there at my ease, cross-legged on deck; after the bitter exertion at the windlass; under a blue tranquil sky; the ship under indolent sail, and gliding so surely along; as I bathed my hands among those soft, gentle globules of infiltrated tissues, woven almost within the house; as they richly broke to my fingers, and discharged all their

opulence, like fully ripe grapes their wine; as I
snuffed up that uncontaminated aroma—literally
and truly, like the smell of spring violets; I declare
to you, that for the time I lived as in a musky
meadow; I forgot all about our horrible oath; in that
inexpressible sperm, washed my hands and my
heart of it; I almost began to credit the old
Paracelsan superstition that sperm is of rare virtue
in allaying the heat of anger; while bathing in that
bath, I felt divinely free from all ill-will, or
petulance, or malice, of any sort whatsoever.

Squeeze! squeeze! squeeze! all morning long; I
squeezed that sperm till I myself almost melted into
it; I squeezed that sperm till a strange sort of
insanity came over me; and I found myself
unwittingly squeezing my co-laborers' hands in it,
mistaking their hands for the gentle globules. Such
an abounding, affectionate, friendly, loving feeling
did this avocation beget; that at last I was
continually squeezing their hands, and looking up
into their eyes sentimentally; as much as to say, —
Oh! my dear fellow beings, why should we longer
cherish any social acerbities, or know the slightest
ill humor or envy! Come, let us squeeze hands all
round; nay, let us all squeeze ourselves into each
other; let us squeeze ourselves universally into the
very milk and sperm of kindness.

Would that I could keep squeezing that sperm
for ever! For now, since by many prolonged,
repeated experiences, I have perceived that in all
cases man must eventually lower, or at least shift,
his conceit of attainable felicity, not placing it
anywhere in the intellect or the fancy, but in the

wife, the heart, the bed, the table, the saddle, the
fire-side, the country, now that I have perceived all
this, I am ready to squeeze case eternally. In
thoughts of visions of the night, I saw long rows of
angels in paradise, each with his hands in a jar of
spermaceti.

I was in the eleventh grade in high school. We were in an
English literature class, a small room with maybe eighteen
students, a teacher who wore her husband's dress shirts,
reading, as I remember, a list of "great books." Specifically, at
the moment, we were reading *Moby Dick*, Herman Melville's
novel about Ahab's insane pursuit of the White Whale. That
day we were focussed on Chapter 94, "A Squeeze of the
Hand," about the whalers on board the Pequod. The crew had
killed a whale, and its carcass had been drawn alongside the
Pequod. Crew members had climbed down onto the whale
floating in the sea next to them and had begun the process of
cutting it up. Their immediate goal was to get the spermaceti
out of the whale into barrels on deck.

What struck me most deeply was the effect of the
spermaceti on Ishmael and the other crew members, the feel of
the spermaceti on their fingers, and the feel of their fingers
touching one another in the barrel of spermaceti, and the
feelings that this touching prompted in him in the very milk
and sperm of kindness.

Sitting in that classroom, at 17 years old, driven nearly
crazy by the conundrum of my sexuality, and feeling that I had
to find something to do with my life, even while my mother
was saying my father's drinking had ruined her life and I was
exactly like him, and that she thought I was headed toward a
wasted, wounded life, I was struck by Melville's ability to
move me, move my feelings, even move my dick to arousal at

17

the thought of holding other men's hands in the tun of spermaceti, and to do this one hundred years after he was dead! I had always been told that I could write. I had written some short stories. I always did well in literature classes. I could write. I thought, I can do what Melville did.

I thought of the enormous power of a writer, his or her ability to affect the emotions and the minds of readers far removed from writers in time and geography. I thought of the tools writers had at their disposal—repetition of words and concepts, metaphor and simile, grammar and punctuation, meter and rhythm. I thought of the immensely long rich history of the literature of my language, all the world's languages coming together and feeding into our own—Latin, Anglo-Saxon, Celtic, German, French, Moorish, African, Russian, East Indian, Spanish, Portuguese, Hebrew, among a host of others—so as to make such a sentence possible *All the multitudinous seas incarnadine, making the green one red*, with its polysyllabic Latinate words playing off against the single syllables of the Anglo-Saxon *making the green one red*. At a time when, as a gay kid, I felt alone and abused and powerless, this immense literature was powerful and was there for me to use. At that time, I was dazzled by American literature, by the great founding documents, by *We hold these truths to be self-evident, that all men are created equal and have certain inalienable rights, and that among these are life, liberty, and the pursuit of happiness,* by the New England transcendentalists, Ralph Waldo Emerson and *Self Reliance*, Nathaniel Hawthorne and *The Scarlet Letter*, Herman Melville and the book that was right in front of me, and by Mark Twain and *Tom Sawyer,* Henry James and his long list of masterpieces —*Portrait of a Lady, The Bostonians, The Golden Bowl*—and in the generation before me, F. Scott Fitzgerald and *The Great Gatsby,* Ernest Hemingway and *For Whom the Bell Tolls, The*

Sun Also Rises, and *A Farewell to Arms,* and, for a Southerner, William Faulkner. Any of us, bookish kids in the South in the late fifties, who were discovering literature just at the moment that Faulkner was publishing his Snopes Trilogy, thought the most compelling possible endeavor to which to devote one's life was writing a book like *The Sound and the Fury.* All of us bookish kids in the South in the late fifties reverberated to Shreve's question and Quentin's answer at the end of *Absalom! Absalom!*—

> "Now I want you to tell me just one thing more. Why do you hate the South?"
> "I don't hate it," Quentin said, quickly, at once, immediately; "I don't hate it," he said. I don't hate it he thought, panting in the cold air, the iron New England dark: *I don't. I don't! I don't hate it! I don't hate it!* (William Faulkner, *Absalom, Absalom!* p. 303)

—as we struggled—and failed—to deal with the world we were inheriting.

Melville called forth in me the emotions that Ishmael felt on board the Pequod squeezing sperm, and it may have been spermaceti that led me to civil rights. He also gave me an exhaustively researched technical treatise on the whaling industry, a sociological treatise on class issues in New England, another about multicultural society in New England in the early nineteenth century, an exciting story filled with suspense which is straight out of *King Kong,* a lesson in geography, all of which is essential to the central story of Ahab, Queequeg, Ishmael, and the White Whale. If it had been technically possible to have tracked the course of the Pequod across the southern Atlantic and Pacific, this story would certainly be huge enough to have been seen from space. Writing a big, long, deeply moving, deeply moral, encyclopedic novel seemed to me to be the very goal I was looking for, but I never considered that it was possible to write about anything truly important that happens on Earth without addressing the deep crimes that men have done to each other. Wars. Slavery. Assassination. Torture. Poverty. Discrimination. Carelessness, Multitudinous forms of oppression. Control of our own bodies. Willful prevention of knowledge. Disenfranchisement. The brutal treatment to which gay men and women have been subjected at the hands of the Christian Church. There is nobody else, no power in the universe, able to make us kill each other but ourselves. And like astronauts getting to the moon then turning around and looking back at ourselves on Earth, it was impossible to see ourselves without seeing where we are in the universe. It would be a willful act of negation to try to write of me—focussing on what I did and how I felt—without taking in what was done to me, and, of course, what I did to them. What is my condition? So I was drawn to a certain kind of life different from all my tribe, even before I had gotten out of high school, and to a certain kind of novel, beginning with a certain kind of physical intimacy, like Ishmael's fingers in the tun of sperm or Queequeg's leg thrown over Ishmael's thigh, *so entirely sociable and free and easy* were we (Herman Melville, *Moby Dick,* Chapter 11, Nightgown).

May 30, 2018

Earthrise 4

During most of my life, there has been only one way to get a manuscript into a format in which everybody can read it, and that is through the publishing industry, owned and operated by large corporations whose expertise is in making money, not literature. They do it by making books and selling them. They do it by thinking in terms of a print-run of, say, 10,000 copies, in which the publisher's income is dependent on how close the publisher comes to 10,000 sold. But it turns out we —those of us alive at this moment—are fortunate to be living in a time of transition, when people are moving to accept ebooks, and print-on-demand books are beginning to match the quality of and the technical achievements of books made on high-speed presses.

I have now published all four of my books in both ebook format, to be read on readers of all kinds, and in print-on-demand format, in which books are printed one-at-a-time as buyers pay for them. This latter is a technology free of the need to sell 10,000 copies of a single print run of a book. One copy, once sold, pays the author more than a great publishing house pays the author for that same copy and pays the printer for his costs and leaves no one else left to be paid. I have written about this moment and its similarity to the invention of moveable type in the fifteenth century and about how both periods were periods of confusion—*why would any community need more than one copy of the Bible?*—and periods of great ferment and growth and the need to educate the book purchaser into a new relationship with books. *I have learned to read, so now I want my own Bible.* I want to concentrate here on the ferment and growth.

These new technologies are already changing the patterns of what gets published and sold and bought and read. New York publishers are no longer the sole gatekeepers to the printed word. Almost eight years ago, I completed the last steps toward creating a digital copy of *Race Point Light.* Yesterday, on Thursday, June 6, 2018, I approved for sale a printed copy of *Race Point Light,* which now can be bought one copy at a time, which purchase completes the sale. Now it's done, and readers have a choice of digital or print editions on all four of my books, and they can also buy them one at a time. They won't go out of print, and I think, when I am dead and my copyright expires, they will move quickly and easily into the world of the public domain.

I don't think we half understand the benefits we are going to reap from these new technologies. These may affect, principally, people on the edges, members like me of a minority whose books have not promised the sales that the big publishers require to stay in business. They are going to have a liberating effect on people in the minorities who want to write about their communities or about something even smaller, something, some aspect of that small community on that small planet in a small solar system far from the center of the universe, but who insist that they be heard. They are going to affect those buyers who want something more liberating than they can get from the local Barnes & Noble. We need not listen to people who say, *Nobody wants to read a book about that,* because somewhere in our cosmos there is a person who wants to read about that, somebody in to something different. Now we have the technology and the commercial model to write, print, and completely pay for that one book at a reasonable price. We don't need 10,000 people to agree to buy the same book to make that book available to the one person— or the ten people— who wants it. This gives millions of separate, distinct individuals who are not part of a large minority access to literature they want without forcing them to resort to the benefit of scale. They don't even have to belong to a minority of two.

The act of writing about Ishmael and Queequeg and Ahab and Moby Dick or the story that Quentin tells Shreve in Cambridge or that John Rechy tells in *City of Night* of his travels through the underbelly of America is an heroic act. On December 10, 1950, William Faulkner gave his speech accepting Nobel Prize for Literature. He says that it is the writer's responsibility to write of "the old verities and truths of the heart, the old universal truths lacking which any story is ephemeral and doomed - love and honor and pity and pride and compassion and sacrifice." Faulkner's list of the "universal truths" should be updated, of course, for the entries on his list are all deeply personal "truths." That list should be expanded to include the conflicts not only of the heart but the conflicts of the polis, the conflicts that arise when the political system does not accurately reflect the reality of the people, when, for example, literature does not accurately reflect people of color and Asian-Americans, women, and Jews and LGBTQ people. *How many novels have you read of young black men fatally shot by cops?* I suggest that pain and courage be added to Faulkner's list of universal truths which are the writer's subject. "I believe that man will not merely endure: he will prevail. He is immortal, not because he alone among creatures has an inexhaustible voice, but because he has a soul, a spirit capable of compassion and sacrifice and endurance. The poet's, the writer's, duty is to write about these things." We can leave the soul for other writers. It is that inexhaustible voice that we need to remember here. LGBTQ men and women and families of color and Asian-Americans and Jews have an inexhaustible capacity for suffering and an inexhaustible well of courage when they confront the ways the polis has oppressed them.

Writing is an heroic endeavor for anyone, but especially for LGBTQ people. We were told that ours was *a love that dare not speak its name*, a belief that effectively eliminated our right to free self-expression, and Blackstone's *Commentaries on the Laws of England,* the basis for American common law, held that the thing that defines us is *not fit to be named among Christians* and *the very mention of which is a disgrace to human nature*. Bill Clinton's administration negotiated *Don't Ask, Don't Tell.* So the act of writing about ourselves—of speaking ourselves out loud—is a defiant deed and a heroic deed, and the more we can gain access to readers without having to go through the gatekeepers of the dominant industry, the more we have liberated ourselves.

We are in the middle of that process now.

June 13, 2018

Earthrise 5

Ceremonies

When my friend Charles Howard was murdered on July 7, 1984, in Bangor, Maine, I had already quit my job teaching and was planning to leave Bangor at the end of the summer, in about two months. After Charlie's murder, and thinking that someone was going to write a book about this—it needed to be written down—I collected a box of flyers and newspaper clippings for the person to use who was going to write the book. In the end, nobody else took up the challenge to write it all down—so I did it, wrote the novel about what happened after Charles Howard was drowned.

1

A novel about a murder of a young gay man can have many shapes. A writer could introduce a man or woman who is a detective who hears about the murder and who begins to investigate, which makes of the novel a detective fiction. Or the novel could be the young gay man's story. He tells us he has had a hard life, difficult relationships with his family, is rootless, a wanderer, abused, wounded. The novel would end with the death of this young man. These approaches use the broad facts of the murder and concentrate in different ways on one person—the detective or the victim. Choosing one or the other of those options is critical to the kind of novel it will be.

But there are other options. What I was moved by was the community of us who came together after our friend was murdered, who got to know each other and to explore our lives together and to learn what we could do to make our lives better —all while we were experiencing initial shock and grief. I realized I wanted to write about this group of us, recognizably a group of us, and also recognizably individuals. I came to understand that the truth that I wanted to write would not be a simple, declarative truth. It would be a truth that was multifaceted, many-colored, iridescent truth and would change from person to person according to generation and gender among those represented in the group of people at the church that night. This would be a kind of conglomerated truth.

The group of us had no leader that summer, so I didn't want to organize the book in such a way that emphasized one person. Or produced one truth. There would be no single narrator to tell this truth. I struggled, at first, looking for a way to organize it, experimenting with third-person omniscient point of view, but then it gradually came to seem right to have each of my characters be his or her own narrator. The reader would not be told one story, he or she would be told a number of different stories which touched on each other in different ways. The story here was the narratives of a number of separate people who for a time accomplished some tasks together and some tasks individually and who frequently contradicted each other. And the result would not be what would happen if you squeezed red paint on a palette, and then blue, and mixed, ending up with purple. What I wanted to see was red, and distinctly separate, blue. And, from a certain distance, a person could begin to see, out of the red and blue, *Un dimanche après midi à l'Île de la Grande Jatte*—but only after a long time and from a great distance.

I began to realize that each character, when he or she began to narrate an episode, would be doing at least two things. Timothy, for example, in his episode, called the Prologue, tells what happened on Saturday, the day of the dance, and he focuses on what they did that day—he and Bernie, which is the name of the boy who is murdered, walk across the bridge, they walk up the hill to Bernie's room, they have sex, they take a nap, they put on makeup, Bernie punches a hole in Timothy's earlobe, they walk through town to the church where the dance will be held. Timothy's narrative also focuses to some degree on the overarching story of the novel, the introduction of the other characters, the basic situation of their group in Cardiff—the fictional name of the city of Bangor—and the death of Bernie Mallett and its immediate consequences. Timothy, sixteen years old, is the gay person who tells us that he saw Bernie die. His last word in this episode is "screaming." The narrative that comes out of Timothy's telling us about himself and about what happens to Bernie, I now began to understand, was going to be messy, unfocussed, confusing, deeply moving, and brilliantly illuminating. And it was going to be contradicted by the next episode. Even aside from being the sole witness to his friend's violent death, Timothy was already victimized in all the ways kids can be victimized. He was sexually abused, he was essentially alone, he was homeless, he had an unspecified learning disability. Each of his parents had rejected him for different reasons, and he was probably an alcoholic. While telling his story, he was also telling the story of homeless LGBTQ youth in town. I wanted to write about a group of individuals who know each other in different ways and in different degrees of intimacy, and who therefore create a dialogue among the LGBTQ people in which, sometimes, one person speaking is answered by another's speaking—and sometimes not. Most often, a person's monologue ignores or pays no attention to anything else that has been said, and one monologue is connected to another monologue only in a reader's mind. The fact of the subject—a group of random LGBTQ people—created the structure of the novel, separate monologues from a random group of people, but joined by the horrific effect of Bernie's death.

I was aware from the beginning that *Ceremonies* would not be an easy read. Reading the text up close can be painful many gay people tell me—they feel the pain like primary colors, undifferentiated and endless—but at a distance, at the distance of purple, they can begin to see other colors. At a distance, the reader, looking at Timothy, would see a boy in harsh pain with strength and courage.

What happened to Timothy, causing him to address his own personal crisis and at the same time to show evidence of a cultural crisis, happens all the way through *Ceremonies* in most of the narratives from the LGBTQ citizens. These people gain an increasingly sophisticated awareness that they are not the only ones being abused, though they are abused in different ways, and they learn how to cope and sometimes to stop it. And they find it very difficult to speak with one voice, leaving the reader of *Ceremonies* the difficult task of finding the narrative.

2

From the moment we came together, it was clear that the men and women in the auditorium of that Unitarian-Universalist Church had unexamined issues with each other. The women, who came from many years of feminist activism, wanted equality with men and recognition of their own abilities and capabilities, and the men, who hadn't paid much attention to all that, wanted equality with straight men. It was clear from the beginning that there were going to be at least two fights going on in the pages of this novel—between gays and straights, and between men and women. The women, who already had years of experience in women's organizations and the advantage of university courses and the whole feminist library of books from writers beginning in the sixties like Germaine Greer, Simone de Beauvoir, Doris Lessing, and later, in the seventies, Adrienne Rich, Del Martin, Alice Walker, Gloria Steinem, Susan Brownmiller, Kate Millett, were impatient with the men who merely wanted to mop up the floor with some straight ass.This conflict among the genders was real, and the divisions went deep and affected everything we did in those months right after Charles Howard was murdered. And, as in the larger conflict, the divisions between men and women exhibited qualities in different people according to their ages, class, ethnicity and geographical origins, and, of course, temperament, education, gender, and family.

3

When I got into the book and made some significant progress, I began to think,*there is very little else out there like this* . My characters were constantly talking about politics and talking in political terms. There were times when characters come together to talk about plans for the next Coalition meeting. They talked about the presidential election, which was ongoing that summer. They talked about the Democratic candidate's choice of a woman for vice-president. They were beginning to see the connection between rejection by a parent, as Mickey is rejected by his mother, and rejection by the President of the United States, who believed, erroneously, that *it is morning in America.* They talked about what laws needed to be passed to prevent another murder of a young gay man. My realization had to do with the fact that I have introduced politics into my book.

Politics, I learned in school in the fifties, has no place in fiction. Jaime Harker has written *Middlebrow Queer: Christopher Isherwood in America*, in which she analyzes the tangled relationships between the government and cultural matters after World War II.

> During the 1940s and 1950s, Cold War intellectuals sought to establish the United States culturally as well as politically (and many did so with covert CIA support for key literary journals). The discipline of American studies— established in books by Leo Marx, F. O. Matthiessen, Richard Chase, and Leslie Fiedler —sought to establish a mythic American spirit; critics in the Partisan Review contrasted the freedom of highbrow aesthetics with the niggardly realism of totalitarian regimes. These cultural interventions were marked by an aggressive masculinity; any deviance was denounced as aesthetically compromised and un-American. Literary criticism implicitly enforced conservative gender roles and betrayed anxiety about inordinate cultural influence of women and gay men in the United States, an anxiety alleviated through prescriptive and narrow literary norms. (Harker, p. 5)

In an essay on *Salon*, "Where's the buzzed-about gay novel?" Daniel D'Addario discusses something he calls "minority lit," in which the minority writer will write, in the words of Alexander Chee, "about the difficulties one faces as X minority in the US—and so this becomes the expectation." Chee concludes, "even before you pick up the novel, it can feel like you're about to read a long-form complaint." In a blog post for this website, "We don't tell the truth about ourselves," I wrote that D'Addario seems to feel that the possibility that a novel is a "long-form complaint" is a terrible thing, driving away publishers and readers. Yet *The Declaration of Independence* is a long form complaint. And so is *Oliver Twist, Bleak House, Intruder in the Dust, Fear of Flying, Mrs. Dalloway, Clarissa,* and virtually every other novel published since *La Princesse de Clèves.* Or, slightly earlier, *The Canterbury Tales* in the fourteenth century. There is very little literature that doesn't have a political thread more or less obviously there for the reader to see. And, of course, the presence or absence of the political thread has nothing much to do with whether or not the fabric is art. As the twentieth century has lavishly shown, art can be made of anything, including a crucifix in Andres Serrano's piss. Despite this overwhelming proof from the whole of twentieth century art, "cold war intellectuals" focussed on one kind of political fiction which was to be guarded against.

As a culture, we've mostly gotten beyond this fear of politics and the blanket rejection of gay-themed literature. But there is a version of this belief which is still around and which still cripples our literature, and this one attacks LGBTQ subject matter from the standpoint of aesthetics. In 2013 Daniel D'Addario interviews Caleb Crain on *Salon*, in a column titled, "The straight canon is very gay." Crain has this to say:

I don't really think that it makes sense for a work of art to take on a social purpose. Just because there are so many constraints that you're working under already — what material is available to you, what your capabilities are with the abilities you have, what will the market bear, what's the nature of your audience — these are the constraints you have to satisfy. If you have a purpose of social reform, I don't think it'd be art.

I also wrote about this column on this blog, *The validity of the lives we lead. adrianabooks.com/blog"*
But sometimes, you can't escape politics. Sometimes, to write about a subject at all means the writer has to take the plunge into politics. Jaimie Harker quotes Christopher Isherwood saying,

> 'There are certain subjects—including Jewish, Negro and homosexual questions—which involve social and political issues. There are laws which could be changed. There are public prejudices which could be removed. Anything an author writes on these subjects is bound, therefore, to have certain propaganda value, whether he likes it or not.' (p.14)

To write honestly of LGBTQ lives is to raise the question in the mind of the reader, *Who or what is responsible for this abuse?* This is an implicitly political question which proposes reform. And yet descriptions of this abuse cannot be considered art, according to Caleb Crain in Daniel D'Addario's article.

Ceremonies is about men and women who were abused and discriminated against in the American republic by American culture. The proof of that lay in the dead body of Bernie Mallett. During the course of the novel much of what people say to each other or say to the reader is to examine just how American culture has abused and discriminated against them. The novel was also about the question *How do we respond?* The reason this was problematic begins with the ancient roots of anti-gay bigotry in Christian Europe. Bigotry in Christian Europe almost always took the form of silencing any attempts to speak out about homosexuality, *the very mention of which,* according to Blackstone, *is a disgrace to human nature.* But there was something much more insidious and dangerous, much closer to the group of LGBTQ people in Maine in the summer of 1984.

What this meant for our purposes was that "cultural interventions" resulted in publishers refusing to publish books which examined the place of homosexuals in American society or which even assumed LGBTQ people had a place in America. As a freshman in college, I worked on the staff of a literary journal which I found later was one of the recipients of the CIA money designed to get the journal to support "conservative gender roles" or "prescriptive and narrow literary norms." I remember getting ready to submit a gay-themed short story to this journal when I was in graduate school, in the sixties, but their advertisement in *The New Yorker* said, "We do not accept any gay-themed stories."

The literary establishment during the fifties and sixties said the lives of LGBTQ people cannot be made into art. We were outsiders and the significant facts about us—the way we had sex and the object of our sexual attraction—meant that the churches, the schools, and the civil authorities all legislated against us. To come out was a political act—we were acting against the culture—and so, apparently, our lives could not be the subject of art. However, knowing that the biggest conflicts and crises of my life have been the consequence of Acts of Congress (the most painful were the consequence of ignorance and stubbornness of members of my own nuclear family), I came to see that if I were to create art out of my life—if I were to tell the truth about my life—it would have to be a political art, in violation of the rules of my culture. On the other hand, every writer on the Stonewall Riots has said that coming out is a political act. "High Art" was the subject Faulkner wrote about and received his Nobel for, and the "old verities" he talked about in his acceptance speech did not include old homosexual pains. But the suffering of LGBTQ persons is a fact about the LGBTQ community that writers cannot ignore when they come to make art out of the lives of LGBTQ persons. I wrote this in 2013 in a post on this blog,

> "Observe the damage these 'Cold War intellectuals'—who took the CIA's money and sought to control the publishing industry to depict only real men—did in the late forties and fifties: a generation or two of gay people savaged by people they thought they could trust, a generation of gay writers whose works were savaged, but most of all, a critical principle repeated so widely that it became everywhere accepted, that gay novels on serious political subjects can be no more than mere propaganda and not in themselves capable of being interesting and compelling literature. We were told, gay art cannot be high art. That's a crime, to have told us that. We'll never know what literature has been lost to us in the last sixty

years because of these 'Cold War intellectuals.'"
Adrianabooks.com/the gay protest novel—1

4

I was determined to write a political novel about the lives of
LGBTQ persons. Since the lives of LGBTQ persons are so
explicitly political, the question, from the beginning, was not
whether but how. There aren't very many LGBTQ novels
about the political condition of LGBTQ people. I suppose that
the short answer is that the writer writes about one subject the
same way he or she might write about other subjects, which is
to say, to the best of his or her ability. The conflict in a political
novel may lie in whether the law is legitimate, in a person's
violation of the law or in how it feels to be subject to the law,
to name a few possibilities. But when considering the pain
LGBTQ men and women have experienced in the last three
thousand years, the politics of their lives lies in their response
to pain, not in whether or not they have suffered.

I knew that it is necessary always to tell the truth. The
writer may lie to his or her reader but must expect the reader to
discover the truth by the novel's end. What the writer cannot
consciously do is lie about the subject of the novel. *I am going
to tell you all about the life of a gay man.* And then, in small
letters at the bottom of the page of the contract between writer
and publisher, *I am not going to put in my novel the fact that
my protagonist's generation would predict that my protagonist
is white hot with rage at being prevented from getting married
to his lover.* Or, *I am not going to tell the reader that my
protagonist has a 32% chance of being infected with HIV.* Or, *a
five-times higher chance of killing himself than the straight
characters in my novel.* If the writer is going to write about a

gay man, he or she must include the fact that LGBTQ persons have been pursued and discriminated against for two or three thousand years. That is, unless you choose at the beginning to write fantasy novels. And if you choose to write fantasy, you should not pretend to be writing realistic fiction. A gay novel which pretends to be realistic which does not include significant information on the effect of bigotry on its characters' lives is a lie.

Our very lives have been, for several thousand years, defined by political and moral oppression. It is clear that the politics of gay people's lives—our oppression by the politics of the majority—are vastly underreported as the subject of literature, so I went ahead with my plans to write the whole story of the consequences of the murder of Charles Howard among the gay community. Then, I thought, when I have finished this very political book, I'll deal with publishing it.

5

It seems that the publishing industry has arranged things so that the subject for gay fiction has to do with sex, which has to do with coming out, and with characters who are fairly young— the age when you come out—and they were not interested in other subjects. But the sex is not what is distinguishing about us. It is that we are legislated against because of the way we have sex. It is the discrimination against us that distinguishes us. And it will always be what distinguishes the generations of LGBTQ people up to now and for the foreseeable future. Even after marriage and the invalidation of sodomy laws and other legal victories, in 2018 we are being told that the appointment of a single new Supreme Court justice may mean the roll-back of our current place in the legal system. Of course, *Moonlight,*

Earthrise 5

Brokeback Mountain, Call Me By Your Name all tell us that coming out is still political, still dangerous, and still here. Neither gay writers nor publishers have yet discovered that gay men and women have lives, which necessarily include a political predicament brought on them by their government.

A legitimate subject of LGBTQ novels is the answer to the question, *How did it feel, to be gay and to be eighteen years old and to be told that you can't serve in the Army? Or work in the State Department?* A legitimate subject of LGBTQ novels is the effect on the community of any number of situations LGBTQ people find themselves in. *The friend of a man who has just been murdered. How did it feel to be in the Stonewall Riots? What did you think about? What if you were in Pulse Nightclub the night of the attack?* How would you feel if you had grown up in the house of your father, Senator Aloysius Beekman, who is a notorious homophobe? *What if your lover—your husband—passed on HIV to you? Or you to him?* What if you had started a novel—the opening sentence is *Happy families are all alike, each unhappy family is unhappy in its own way*—and you planned for the novel to be about three gay men, two of whom are in a difficult relationship into which the third is insinuating himself? These—and many more—are the questions that need to be asked and answered in our literature about a gay man living on that small planet floating around a small star in a distant corner of the cosmos falling through space. The way these questions are answered is—or ought to be—a major part of our literature. Our thoughts and feelings about these questions, and about the hundreds of other questions, are what make our lives matter on this small planet and are the raw material out of which comes an answer to the question, *How is it for you there on that small planet?* We must be able to say, before we die, *I lived here, and I felt this, and*

Earthrise 5

my name is Timothy. I am sixteen years old. Straight people
have this kind of literature. I want it for us, too.

July 7, 2018

Earthrise 6

Ceremonies: Who were these people?

1

Timothy tells us. He's sixteen, he's a male, he's gay, he's homeless, he does tricks on "the hill" to get money, he hangs out with an older kid, Bernie, he has sex with Bernie sometimes, he knows Claire who has spiked hair and wears a leather bracelet with steel studs, he also knows Mickey and Mickey's lover Robbie, and Derek, the actor. He mainly talks about things 16 year-old kids talk about—*How can I get a boyfriend? Are they going to hurt me?* Timothy says, "My mom says I'm nothing but a pain and a heartache to her."—and then occasionally he breaks out of all that when Bernie says to him, "Someday I'll have a man in love with me, and he'll give me a garden." Timothy answers, "You're queer. And you live in a rooming house and you don't have a garden and you don't have any money and no way to get one. And that's the way it's going to be for you all your fucking life." He's deep inside his own life—the details of it—and then suddenly he breaks out and hugely expands the scope of his vision. *I know what a queer is, and I know the conditions of his life and its limitations.*

We meet Timothy, who knows other gay kids, whom we get to know at the dance they all go to—it's a group of kids who've pushed back the chairs in a church auditorium and found a record player and are dancing with each other. The reader gets to know a few of the kids—Mickey the computer guy, Robbie the dancer, Jack and a few others. We meet Claire and Marybeth. Then we follow the events that lead up to Bernie being murdered and to Timothy reaching through the railing on the side of the bridge toward the water where Bernie is drowned. After Timothy, we meet Carole, and then we meet Mickey, speaking for himself, which begins the process of our meeting Dana, Channing, Derek, Luke, Marybeth, Perry, Deborah, and Luke, some of them for the second time. Most of these people tell a story that is a self-contained narrative. Luke does it twice, once in the middle of the day Sunday and once late at night at the end of Monday night, which ends Part 1. By the time Deborah starts talking, it begins to be clear that there is a small group of gay people in Cardiff of various ages who are going to be part of this story. Some of them knew Bernie, and some didn't. They come back in the second part, and again in the third.

As each of the narrators in *Ceremonies* come forward, they start off situating themselves—their personal selves—in the community in Cardiff, and then, almost coincidentally, almost by accident, they expose what they know of bigger matters— the murder of the strange kid from out of town, the place of LGBTQ people in American culture, What is life like? Carole, whose episode is the first after Timothy's Prologue, starts off saying, *I'm all right as I am.* She's sitting in the church (right side of the aisle) on Sunday morning, in the largest, oldest Catholic church in town, observing the stained glass windows, which are "famous." The priest, who is a "fool," according to

Carole, is "blathering on," and then Carole notices a woman sitting two rows ahead of her and to the left. It's Deborah, who is 48, two years older than Carole, and loves the priest, and called this morning about a small article in the paper about a man drowning last night in the Passadumkeag Stream. "He was naked, it seems," Carole says. So, all of a sudden, all of Carole's quiet satisfaction with herself is thrown into turmoil by this woman Deborah and her news from a small article from the inside of the paper, and then later Sunday as they talk on the phone and still later when Deborah comes to Carole's house. During the rest of Carole's episode, Deborah keeps intruding, bringing more and more painful and tragic news— that is, she brings what is merely the news of her life. She's a librarian and a teacher, and she taught Timothy at one point. Carole closes with a comment about Deborah. "She said when she left she was going home to watch the news. How grotesque. What does she have to do with him! Wild animals and demons. God, it makes me so angry….Europe. I'll go to Europe. My passport is up to date and in the safety deposit box at the bank. I must find a bricklayer who can build a brick wall, something high, and all around my garden."

There are, throughout *Ceremonies*, episodes of different narrators, some of whom the reader will hear from again, and some of whom will narrate one episode and then not be heard from again.

2

The "wall" that she daydreams of suggests that Carole is not open to the huge changes that are in the near future for most of the other characters. Mickey, for example. He has his good job, he has computer skills that make him valuable on the job market, he has a decent apartment, he has a boyfriend, and many of the gay kids in Cardiff are in and out of his apartment, coming in, watching tonight's news of the death of Bernie Mallett, staying for supper, sleeping overnight. Maybe it is the fact that Mickey is embedded in the group of young people, maybe it is the kind of person Mickey is, maybe it is just how different Mickey's circumstances are when compared to Timothy and Carole—everybody knows him and he is already out to some degree, at least among his gang—but even though Mickey is distressed by Bernie's death and by how much his friends are suffering and by his own grief, he demonstrates that he is open to what the future is going to bring. In his last words, leaving the gym where he has met Robbie, he says, "I am very strong," and, of Robbie he says, "he is very handsome."

Mickey—and Dana and Deborah and Derek and Marybeth and Luke—all go through journeys of a sort, learning from Bernie's death, each with his or her own questions. The longest episode—53 pages—in *Ceremonies* is Mickey's, in Part 2. The shortest—two pages—is Channing's, in Part 2. Such an arrangement invites the reader to care about the character or situation of the various people in *Ceremonies,* and to ask the question of them, *The death of Bernie Mallett changes everything. Who is going to resist change? Who is going to be part of the change?*

While most of the single-episode narrators are constrained in some way and unable to respond to the murder of Bernie Mallett except with anger or fear, there are several characters who have only one episode each who place the events going on around them in the context of the national gay community and who aren't themselves susceptible to change, usually because they are already ahead of the curve of their peers in Cardiff.

Earthrise 6

The man in the episode at the beginning of Part 3, called Craig, is driving north on I-95 toward Millinocket, going into the woods for a week of camping, talking about Bernie's death and the consequent political activity in Cardiff. Craig says, "These people are dealing with issues the rest of us dealt with in 1970." Craig and his friend are LGBTQ activists who live in Boston, where they have been active for three or four years in AIDS organizations—AIDS Action, and ACT-UP. There is another narrator who has one episode who is carrying on an active and varied sex life, who seems to be balanced and stable and who seems untouched by the murder of Bernie Mallett. His job is not threatened, his family is not affected, and his social group is not affected. His episode is in exactly the center of the novel. There are a few others.

3

The novel is divided into three parts—the run-up to the memorial service near the end of Part 1, the middle part in which the Coalition has trouble getting its act together, which ends with Dana's vision of total freedom, and Part 3 in which there are three separate resolutions—the School Committee Meeting, the national election in November, 1984, the Gay Pride March in 1984—plus an Epilogue, which provides a different resolution still. The novel, therefore, has a climax at the end of Part 1, a second climax at the end of Part 2, a third climax after Part 3, and then the Epilogue.

These climaxes are increasingly important—the first is four hundred people gathered in a church for a memorial service and then walking down the hill to the Kenduskeag Stream, where Bernie Mallett died. This climax at the end of Part 1 is personal, the characters focussed on their grief, and their emotions are on broad display. Deborah also focusses on her

43

memories of the evening she and Betsey walked along the Kenduskeag Stream, holding hands, what happened there, and her encounter with the police, the intense and profound feelings of humiliation and shame and anger and rage. Luke, at the very end of Part 1, in a kind of coda, remembers the ways his mother humiliated him, his memories still with him 65 years later. At the end of Part 2, in the climax, the characters move on to something deeper—to questions that now have to be answered. *What are we? What is an LGBTQ person? What do we want? Is it freedom? Is that it?* It's the kind of dialogue that a group would have who are drenched in metaphysics and willing to pursue their discussion wherever it leads. At the end of Part 3, Luke goes to the School Board Meeting, the local city response to the murder, and listens while the citizens and some of the coalition members try to describe what it is about America and its gay people that the one should tolerate the other. They can't do it. Then Dana remembers Gay Pride in Boston in 1984 four months ago and people she met there and the posters she saw there and the balloons—as Dana says, *lavender for the living and green for the dead.* And then Dana is waiting in line to vote in the 1984 election. The reader of course knows the outcome of that election, and having read 532 pages that covered most of what happened in Cardiff since Bernie Mallett drowned, she knows how critical that election—and any presidential election—is. How universally important. The election registrar, looking at the register of voters, looks up at Dana, smiles, and finding Dana's name in the list, says, "There you are!" She smiles at Dana. And Dana herself smiles back. She says, "Here I am!" It has been a long journey. Then the Epilogue with Derek, with its existential struggle over gender, with its presentation of the source of all conflict in *Ceremonies.*

4

A thread runs through the whole of *Ceremonies*, like the omnipresent political theme, and that is the concept of sexuality. *Why do so many people differ over our understanding of it? What causes it? What makes one respond sexually in one way or another?* The Bishop of Portland says that it is necessary to remember that "these people" commit sin every time they have sex, a rigid and reductive way of conceptualizing sexuality. Dana refers to Kinsey and seems drawn to the idea that sexuality, as a way of categorizing people, is going to wither away as people find it less and less descriptive of their lives. Marybeth and Mickey and Deborah and Luke all seem directed by their sexuality to fight back against their culture. Vernon has a similar sexuality but does not feel driven to do anything except look for ass. He seems at peace with his sexuality and generally at peace with his culture.

Fighting back is apparently just about the only thing that Jack is driven to do. The group in *Ceremonies* is large enough to make the point that Luke makes early on, *We are everyone.* The narratives emphasize the varieties of same-sex sexual experiences. Perry, for example, seems in stiff pain in his marriage, and another man in very similar circumstances is relaxed and at ease with himself and his life. There are men who are basically in to same-sex but who have chosen to express that desire in an other-sex marriage. More variety, more difference, more recognition of the infinite number of ways humans can couple, and consequently, of the infinite number of ways humans can resist being imprisoned by their culture.

5

The most powerful factor that drove the writing of *Ceremonies* and drove the structure of the resulting book and its length and the depth to which it dives into its subject, is the pain experienced by the lesbian and gay and bisexual and transgender and queer persons caused by American culture. There were two lodestars that I was aware of that were on every page of this novel and that I never lost sight of, and those were the pain that most LGBTQ persons grow up with and live with every day of their lives, and the power of forces that have created the culture that caused the pain and killed Bernie Mallett. This does not mean that LGBTQ persons, to free themselves, must reject all their culture or destroy their culture, but it does mean that LGBTQ persons, to free themselves, must have the power to reject those aspects of the culture that reject them or to alter their culture to make it more accommodating to LGBTQ persons, and it must be the LGBTQ persons who decide which segments they will reject or alter.

6

Ceremonies is not finally a novel about coming out, although most of the characters in the novel do come out during the course of the novel. It is, instead, about the formation of a community of persons who discover that they have to come out. "Ceremonies"—all the little ceremonies of life, of the LGBTQ community, of hospitality, of sex, of initiation— demonstrates that they are a member of a community and are not alone.

While the drive is toward forming a community, still the greatest impact of *Ceremonies* is in its emphasis on the individual LGBTQ citizen of Cardiff. The range of different kinds of citizens suggests the range of possibilities and options for LGBTQ citizens of Cardiff. *Ceremonies* is a refutation of concepts like "the gay," with its implication that there is such a thing as a gay person or that all LGBTQ persons are alike. We are a multitude, to use Walt Whitman's word— men and women, white and black, kids and aged persons, closeted and out—within the range of the possibilities of Cardiff.

7

When I first began to think about *Ceremonies,* I thought it was necessary for LGBTQ persons to write it down. That is, it is important for us to record our history in real time, for the people who lived it to write down what they experienced so that in the future LGBTQ persons will have an accurate record of what life has been like for gay persons. Writing it down is an act of defiance. The single most important means that the dominant culture has employed to keep LGBTQ persons down is to keep us from expressing the things we know about ourselves. I have brought this up a number of times in these Earthrise blogs. We've all been told, *Don't speak, we will speak for you and we will tell you what you are.* For seventeen years, we were told, *Don't ask, Don't tell.* I would think that almost every single LGBTQ person has learned at some point that he or she was not to talk about this. This means that, in each generation, much of what we know has been lost to us. Since a gay person carries in his or her body no DNA that connects him or her as a gay person to any other gay person on Earth, and since few gay people are born into gay families— although more are being born into gay families every day—it is critical for us to learn how to pass on what we know so that we are not forever trapped in repeating again and again the single subject *coming out.* The answers are out there. Movies, novels, books, poetry, scientific studies like Kinsey's, painting, data collection, almost any way that human activity can be recorded can tell us what has happened to us. It has only been in the last fifty or sixty years that we have been able to trust some of the scientific studies of us. Even today many supposedly scientific studies are actually studies flawed by the bigotry of the scientist. They ask questions like, *What causes homosexuality?* So their answers have to do with *What went wrong?* They should ask the question, *What gene or genes cause sexual attraction?* We could take these things one at a time and show how they have failed us. One will suffice. While the number of movies on LGBTQ-themed subjects grows almost daily, it has still been only fifty or sixty years (since the release of a movie like *Reflections in a Golden Eye*) that the big studios have begun to deal with LGBTQ issues at any depth, and much less than that that they have dealt with these issues at sufficient depth. I have already said that I don't think movies have yet even begun to scratch the surface of the LGBTQ material that is there. There is no queer *8 1/2,* no queer *Nashville*, no queer *Alien,* no queer *Bladerunner,* and we know that Ennis Del Mar's life didn't end when he looks at the postcard of Brokeback Mountain. What about the other forty years of his life? Has nobody found anything about those forty years that ought to be made into a movie? Can nobody conceive of anything that Ennis could do or experience that could make those forty years important to us? Or critical to our understanding of ourselves and of him? Like most writers, movie producers have a narrow view of LGBTQ lives. We have beautiful movies, some of them very moving, of one beautiful man falling in love with another beautiful man, or of a beautiful boy coming out. And not much else. No *Casablanca.* No *West Side Story.* There are brief scenes, there are suggestions, there are hints and coded signals, but no big movie where the tragedy of being LGBTQ is treated as seriously as the tragedy of being straight.

Independent of anything else, I felt a strong personal obligation to write down what I knew of Charles Howard's death. He only lived in Bangor, Maine, for about two months, and I only knew him during those months. I have children and my presumption was my children would have children, and I knew that they would grow up in a world with LGBTQ people. I owed it to them to give them what I knew. One generation may use any of those modes listed above—movies, novels, books, poetry, scientific studies like Kinsey's, painting, data collection, almost any way that human activity can be recorded can tell us what has happened to us—or as many of these modes as is convenient to pass on what is important about their lives to the next, newer, generation. But it can't keep what it knows bottled up. It must learn what there is to learn from the preceding generation and then do its part to pass on what it knows to younger people. And it won't do to say, *We have marriage, so we have reached the end of history and from now on it is just fun and games.*

The record we leave of ourselves is the respect we pay to Charles Howard and Matthew Shepard and Oscar Wilde and the hundreds of thousands of others who have died of abuse, as well as to ourselves. It is our way of saying, *We will not ignore what happened to you, and to Leonard Matlovich and the millions who have died of AIDS*, it is our way of saying, *We haven't forgotten you.* To record our lives in this way is to assert our value and our contribution to life on Earth.

July 23, 2018

Earthrise 7

Race Point Light

This novel begins in Provincetown, out on the end of Cape Cod, and ends in Provincetown sixty years later. It has one narrator, who sticks with the task all the way through the novel, and it has one subject—the narrator's life—and one focus, the narrator's life as a gay man. It begins when the narrator is about two, and it ends when the narrator is about sixty-five. Along the way, he deals with ignorant teachers, the hostility of other students, marriage, alcoholism, divorce, the LGBTQ community in the time of AIDS, the deaths of many of his friends, and the questions of gay kids. His life is like most lives. It has the standard crises and traumas and the standard successes—his children, some aspects of his marriage to a woman, his marriage to a man, the survival of some of his friends. Life, for him, is incredibly rich. As he grows older and receives experience and education, he comes to understand that very very little of his life has been wasted. At the end, he feels that all of his experience has brought him to this moment, has prepared him for it, and has enabled him to make the best of it.

Earthrise 7

1

While writing *Ceremonies,* I occasionally wanted to extend my attention on a character beyond the limits set by the requirements of the novel I was writing. I think the reader knows the direction Mickey's life is going to take when he walks out into the cold that November night in 1984, Robbie on his arm. But sometimes, in similar situations, I have wanted to take the character and ask more of her. Take Marybeth, for example. Her world is much newer than Mickey's, and so at the end of her last episode, with the word *gold*, we know less of her world than of Mickey's. I would like to have had more time—and space—to devote to her life. Would a commune really be the long-term solution to the issues raised by the novel? If not, what would an enormously well-educated and sophisticated and experienced woman propose in its place? It may be that she has the answer to the future that seems to elude many of the others.

I was drawn to the idea of writing a book, perhaps of the same length as *Ceremonies*, and structured by close attention to the activities and feelings of one person and also to the effect of governments at various levels on the people. I wanted this book focused on a single person, where I was not limited by a period of time like that between July 7, 1984 and election night, November 6, 1984, even with flashbacks. Having lived through the forties and fifties and sixties, I was aware that there have been very few books written about LGBTQ men who have lived through those decades. The books that have been written have been essentially coming out narratives. The significant social change that happened during that period were the Stonewall Riots and their consequences. Before the riots, there was no option other than heterosexual marriage for LGBTQ people. After the riots, there was gay activism. And there were people who went from a heterosexual marriage to gay activism. This was, in fact, what I did.

But the way that shift was explained was off-putting for many people. A guy was in a marriage to a woman because there was, apparently, no other option, and then the Stonewall Riots gave him another option, so he decided to be honest about himself and come out. It's the *be honest about himself and come out* that I resist. Many of us who were married were entirely honest about ourselves all the way through our marriages. And there were many reasons for getting-married-though-gay. There might have been some people who were so frightened of being gay that they fled into the protection of a straight marriage. But all the people I knew who got married knew full well that they had same-sex desire and felt no particular fear or disgust at it, but, if they also knew they could achieve erections in other-sex sex, this provided them a solution whose only other option was a lifetime without any intimate contact. And when they decided to get a divorce, it was not a case of their *now* being willing to be honest with themselves, it was a case of the culture having given them an option which was not available when they had first gotten married to a woman.

If I go to any large gathering of LGBTQ persons, I can see that there are many people who have been married. Particularly older LGBTQ persons. When I was young, I was told by psychologists and psychiatrists that their goal was to "cure" me. If this was not stated clearly, it was implicitly assumed. From my marriage in 1965 to 1969, the dominant message that was being given to LGBTQ persons was to *get married.* As my mother said, "Find a lovely girl and settle down." And I did that because I was a good boy. And I lived with the lovely girl for eighteen and a half years, and there was no time during those years when I ever lied to myself or, for that matter, to anyone else.

2

The other thing I learned from my own life was that I never quit anything and then started something new. I had a life, and it went on and on, through my education at various levels, through my service in the Army, graduate school, marriage to a woman, teaching in the Midwest, teaching in New England, writing in Boston, marriage to a guy. There was no way to take part of that life, one segment of that life, and make it the whole of the plot of a novel. At least until our culture has developed LGBTQ literature enough so that we have many many novels which present the whole of LGBTQ people's lives to read from, we need to focus on the fact that gay people have whole lives, from childhood to great age, and coming out is not the only segment of that life nor the most important. What I did at twelve affected me at 29 and 50 and now at 79. The difference between another kind of novel—where the writer focuses on the years of the breakup of his marriage to a woman, and then tells of the narrator's younger years in flashback—is that what I wanted to write was a novel in which the writer had not already chosen which segment of the narrator's life was the most important. Was it his heterosexual period? His homosexual period? The shift between the two? Is it even possible to write about a life which has two segments? I have children, who are beautiful and talented and hard working, and I have spoken to both of them in the last 48 hours, and it is impossible now to say that I used to be straight, and that now I am gay. There are many hundreds of thousands of people who are one thing and then do the major thing identified with the other. I have said in *Race Point Light* that our whole intellectual structure around sexuality has not fit our lived reality since, at least, Kinsey's *The Sexual Behavior of the*

Human Male in 1949. We keep learning, for example, that there are more than two genders, and yet we still keep talking about men and women, gay and straight. *It is enough to make a guy think he should write a book.*

3

I structured *Race Point Light* around my own life, but it's a novel. It is, first, not all of my life. I focussed on the principal character, the narrator, as he is a gay man in a culture that hates gay people. My narrator is an academic, but I cut out all of his life except those parts of his life that affected his sexuality. That still left plenty of material for me to use in this book, but having cut so much material, it is hard to call it a memoir or an autobiography. There are several sexual scenes in the novel that never happened, and several that did, and several characters who don't exist in life. There are also a number of people who had major parts to play in my life but who don't appear in *Race Point Light*. I don't have the same configuration of siblings the narrator does in *Race Point Light*, nor do I have siblings with the same gender as the narrator. The point here is that this novel really is a novel and tells the reader nothing he can count on that could turn it into autobiography. And what it is, is a novel about something near the whole of a gay man's life who lived from about 1940 and 2004. It has climaxes—the end of his education, for example, his decision to marry, his failure to get tenure at the University of Michigan, his quitting his next job at the University of Maine, then a climax at a viewing of The Quilt, and, finally, a walk the length of Commercial Street, in Provincetown, Cape Cod—and I think it keeps you reading, but it's a sad 200 pages that end the book. It's the time of AIDS, and there are many deaths.

4

When I wrote this book and started trying to publish it, I began
to get the response from publishers that I should break it up,
publish it in two volumes to make it easier for the publishers to
make their money back. Selling two 300-page volumes at
$25.00 each was more advantageous to a publisher than selling
a 600-page volume at $25.00 each. My book was a serious gay
novel with little sex, much suffering, and the publishers didn't
think it would sell many copies. They thought they had a better
chance of making their money on it if it were in two volumes.
However, splitting it up broke up the central goal I had
established for it—one narrative about a gay man who married
a woman and then, later, married a man and whose life made a
coherent whole. The natural place to split it into two books was
at the end of Part 4, where Andy dies, which would have left
me with two volumes, the first of which presented the narrator
in a heterosexual life and the second a gay life. The split would
have emphasized the narrative many of us tell ourselves about
our lives: *We are straight and then we are gay, when we start
being honest with ourselves.* I was not going to give in to that,
even at the possibility of losing a publishing contract. In my
book, the narrator was honest with himself all the way through.
The task was to make the parts of the book that didn't have to
do with coming out as interesting as the more familiar parts
that did have to do with coming out.

5

To do so, I altered my source material in a number of ways.
I cut back the size of my family, reducing the size of my
mother's family down to one aunt and almost eliminating my
father's family. Later in the book, I completely eliminated the

narrator's lover's family. I wanted the finished book to focus strongly on what it felt like at family gatherings to be a gay kid amid all these heterosexuals. Then I allowed the one aunt to have only two children, not the four or five children each of my aunts and uncles actually had, who merely confused and caused the basic plot to be out of focus. This clarified the structure of the novel and kept the reader's attention on the basic conflict— gay kid among all these heterosexuals. I didn't need to repeat over and over the fact that it was difficult to grow up gay among all these heterosexuals—each time with a different family. Now this time with the narrator's mother's second sister's family. They all functioned the same, so I cut them out. Although many members of my family thought I was working on a novel about my family, *Race Point Light* was never about my family. It was about a gay man growing up in a conservative, religious homophobic family and then leaving that family and going away and creating distance from them in another culture, and then learning how to cope. I kept doing this. I moved to Michigan from my native South Carolina, seeking another way to live, then I moved to Maine, each time looking for a place that enabled my social, sexual, and intellectual needs to be addressed. This search is fairly closely followed in *Race Point Light*. On the other hand, I kept my children largely out of the narrative that made up *Race Point Light*. I didn't want to create a portrait of either one of them that then was fixed and beyond their control to change as they grew older. They were their lives. Finally, there was my husband. While I could not have written *Race Point Light*, or *Winter Rain*, or *Adam in the Morning*, without his support and did write them with his support, the portrait of him in *Race Point Light* is a partial one, suggestive rather than definitive. The same was true of other areas of the narrator's life.

What is important in some periods of his life disappear and let other issues take their place in later periods. It is also true that he deals with the conflicts of his life in a different way than he dealt with them earlier.

6

Race Point Light is the same kind of novel as *Ceremonies*. It is deeply political, its analyses include an analysis of the national political scene, including the national parties, and it includes state and local commentary, its major characters are conflicted over political issues—all of them having to do with the LGBTQ community—that arise out of national and state and local political struggles. From almost the first scene in the garden in Columbia, the principal LGBTQ narrator is aware of national politics and its effect on him. In a major way, the novel is political—independent of political parties or elections —in that the narrator is aware of his community and his place in it and his need to resolve its conflicts. The principal character in *Race Point Light*, even though he describes himself as a loner and "alone," is still a person who gathers people around him and seeks to create a community or to better the one he has. His whole method is that of a political leader, and while he experiences deeply personal pain at significant times in his life, still his tendency is not to seek out a therapist but to seek out or to make himself available to people. He seeks to find a way to live in which he is respected, and to endeavor to earn the respect of his community, and he resists for years the need to rebel. His work is for the polis and for the betterment of the polis.

When Fair Shaw and Tim visit The Quilt when it is brought to Boston, the two men try to sort out what Shaw will put on Tim's quilt when it comes time. They toy with various

58

expressions as they walk around the arena floor, looking at the quilts of the dead. Finally, Tim says, "I have it. Put on my quilt, *He worked to bring about the collapse of Western Culture.*" This ends the first part of the final 225-page-section of the book dealing with Boston and AIDS. Since the time spent on the arena floor has been spent examining the failures of American culture during the AIDS epidemic, I think Tim's suggestion is correct, and it is certainly consistent with Shaw's ideas in the rest of the book. The culture needed a radical restructuring in the wake of AIDS and the failures of the Reagan and the Bush administrations. Eventually, it almost got it, in the Presidency of Barack Obama.

This is exactly the point of contention between my goal for *Race Point Light* and those "Cold War intellectuals" who said that politics did not belong in literature. Plague has always been a subject for art. The Isabella Stewart Gardner Museum in Boston held an exhibition on World AIDS Day called Art's Lament, in which paintings from the Middle Ages were united with contemporary paintings and photographs prompted by the AIDS crisis to form the subject of the exhibition. A small figurine eight inches high of a grieving woman, chosen by a curator at the Museum of Fine Arts in Boston as a way of marking World AIDS Day, became a political object when it is understood that it was a virus that killed, not God's will. Our political tools become willpower, money for research, expert scientists, rather than prayer. And the solution to the crisis lies in some sort of collective action. In our time an artist of any kind cannot write or draw or compose or dance his or her art prompted by AIDS without being political. In a larger sense, we cannot create art out of the lives of LGBTQ persons without creating political art, just because our lives have been made political by churches, religions, political parties, educators, and "Cold War intellectuals," and by the fact that our lives were already political when we arrived on the scene, and if we are going to create art out of life, it will be political art. Ours is a democratic age, and the response of the reader to a work of political art is to be moved to act. The reader may choose not to read or see or attend the performance of a particular work of art, but we must be clear. He or she is limiting himself or herself to a partial vision. Choosing not to accept the reality of political art is like choosing not to write about ambitious people, or about sex-driven people, or about particularly talented sculptors, or about people who write books. It is a refusal to read about us and about our lives.

7

I have always liked the question, *How is it for you there?* when trying to explain what any of my novels are about. *How is it for you there?* there, where you are in Bangor, Maine, on July 7, 1984, or in any of the places Fair Shaw lives during the last decades of the twentieth century, or at 2:00 AM on the morning of June 28, 1969 on Christopher Street in Greenwich Village. I wanted, within the parameters of my subject, to give everything that could answer the question, *How is it for you there?* I wanted to establish where the narrator is—where on Earth—and then where he is in his life, how old he is, whether his marriage is a good one, to a man or a woman, where his happiness comes from, and, as important, all the sources that produce his anxiety and stress and anger and his love. This is particularly important in *Race Point Light*, where Fair Shaw experiences anxiety, for example, from different sources, and it is necessary to sort them out to know what is seriously threatening and what is mere cultural noise, and, consequently, how seriously the narrator's attacks on his culture are to be received.

Earthrise 7

I suppose my reader may sometimes be overwhelmed by how much I give him or her, and be tempted to throw the book across the sands with the exclamation, "What the fuck!" but all the information I give the reader is essential to arriving at an answer to the question, *How is it for you there?* which is another way of saying, *This is what this novel is about.*

July 28, 2018

Earthrise 8

Race Point Light

What kind of person is Fair Shaw? Only partially like me, I should say at the beginning. Taller, darker, handsome, certainly sexier, that long dolorous list of qualities that show we don't measure up. I think he is more in control of his emotions than I am, less resentful, less angry, more charming. More athletic. Because, at seven, being athletic on the playground is about the biggest achievement there is, a failure there stayed with a boy —a man—all the rest of his life. A few other men seem to be able to achieve success at seven, savor it, and then move on, forgetting about it, never again thinking about dodgeball for the rest of their lives. But for those who fail, it is like a brand on the forehead. *He can't catch a ball.* So, I conceive of Fair Shaw as a better, more successful me, and I would guess that is about what other writers do who base a character on themselves. I made him like me—but better. Mainly what I wanted him to be was less confused. I remember being confused for whole years at a time when I was growing up, and while I understand that confusion in the hero of a novel has a certain charm, I get the sense that mainly writers ought to stay away from it. I sense that writers who are good at confusion also have a light touch at writing about emotions, and I don't think I do.

1

What I was mainly confused about was sex—was it bad or good?—were my parents right or were my feelings right about it? And then, should I do what my parents wanted me to do—cut my hair, tuck my shirt in, get a belt—or do what I wanted to do, which was to look like the rough kids from school, or *kiss him*. What I was good at was being good at my studies, and nobody but the teacher thought that was very admirable. I was real confused about that. Now that I am an adult and have been an adult since John F. Kennedy was elected president, I am not confused, but I can remember.

I focus on the narrator's feelings. The problem I had was to find a way to have the narrator start off the novel confused, start off not knowing, start off hurting, and then to show that he is gradually narrowing his focus. Instead of thinking that grownups were a little mysterious and talked about things the children didn't understand, I came finally to see that I understood more than the grownups did. The trick was to focus. As long as I was unclear about what I wanted, as long as I was going to say that my ignorance was total, then I was going to remain ignorant. But when I was able to say, *I need to find out about masturbation,* then I can get that myself or I could just play around with it until I had the goods. If you focus, you can be less ignorant. If you ask the right people the right question—one question—you may be able to get the right answer, even if you're just a kid.

2

Once I started paying attention to my own behavior—the

behavior of my own body—and I put that together with what I overheard at school, I made more progress. I connected the sight of other boys' naked bodies with what was happening to my penis, then with what I was hearing from the other boys. There were places I couldn't go to get information on sex. I was embarrassed to go to the library. I had an afternoon job, which was downtown, near the State House and across the street from the largest public library in the city, and I knew I could go there, but the people who worked there knew me. It was part of my job to go to the library and get reports on government things, so everybody at the library knew me. I couldn't go into that library and have somebody see me looking up "homosexual." And there was nobody else at other places to ask. What I'd get back was, "What are you asking about that for?" I couldn't ask a priest, and I didn't know any doctors. I knew the lifeguard at a lake club outside of town whose tight hard body in even tighter swim trunks turned me on, and he gave me an unmistakable declaration, *You're a homosexual,* without even saying the words.

I learned what homosexual meant from listening to kids and reading the newspaper and reading magazines. I could go downtown to the Capitol News Stand and see the magazines for homosexuals. Handsome guys with blond slicked-back hair and muscles in tight swimming suits. I learned I was a homosexual, too, and without giving away anything about me. So I was not only learning about what homosexuality was, I was learning how homosexuals acted. Like me. Secretively. I was still thinking that maybe my culture—what everybody called society—might be right about homosexuals, but they couldn't be right about the other part of it, what they were doing to me. Every other sin or crime or failing in the world could be talked about except this one, and this one caused a scandal just reading about it in the library. I learned that they kept books on it locked up. My aunt wanted them to censor a British movie of *Tom Jones* because it had too much sex in it. My father bought *The Sexual Behavior in the Human Male* when it came out, and he laughed at my aunt. At first I hadn't known about political inclinations. Then I discovered my father was very conservative, and I found out later he was actually a libertarian. He didn't think censorship was right in any case, and he didn't feel any artist should face any control from the government. Later, I didn't remember him saying anything about queers, but he was adamantly opposed to the censorship of *Ulysses*. He had great respect for the written word. He was a recovering alcoholic, and Mother said that, while you can't inherit alcoholism, you can inherit the "tendencies." And she thought I had them. I thought that whatever was happening was my fault. I came to understand that it wasn't my fault, it was really that my family was fucked up with alcoholism and a bunch of other things, and while my dad was a good man and respected literature and didn't think the government should be allowed to censor anything, still he lived in a world which simply didn't know anything about homosexuality. Now if he had known something about it, he might have come down on the right side of all this. But he didn't, and he didn't, and so while we both loved seventeenth century lyric poetry, we never had a conversation about my being queer. Mother, on that subject, was a disaster. But it was decades before I was sure that my culture was wrong about homosexuality and that it was OK to be gay.

3

The conflict between queer and straight, which seemed to

dominate my life, was also illustrated almost everywhere else. One of the images from my childhood was of my great-uncle's place outside of Charleston, on the Ashley River, it had been a plantation a long time ago and had an avenue of live oak trees leading to a large white frame house with black shutters. It called up a host of daydreams and fantasies of the pre-Civil War South with images of masters and slaves. It also called up ideas of John Locke's original charge from Charles II of England which resulted in Locke's writing *Two Treatises of Government,* which eventually, one hundred years later, influenced Thomas Jefferson when he wrote the *Declaration of Independence,* with its words, *All men are created equal.* The sharp conflict between *slaves* and *created equal,* which was buried deep in the national psyche, was also buried deep in my psyche. I was aware of it, and I struggled with it—the idea of slaves being inextricably linked with the idea of my own family, who had been slave-owners in the pre-Civil War South, and the need to be equal, as I grew up and grew older, being equally inextricably linked with my being gay. The site of this struggle was my own brain, where I struggled for mastery between the images that my family represented—slavery—and the concepts my education and my reading and my own thoughts presented me with, which were freedom and equality. This mental conflict is a thread running through *Race Point Light* from Fair Shaw's childhood into his forties, when he at last so decisively rejects his family that he was also able to decisively reject their baggage too.

The conflict between what the nation had actually experienced, and what the brain produced as the result of DNA, suggested a direction my novel would take. Between Shaw's family and his sexuality, it was inevitable that Shaw would submit to his sexuality. "Family" does not control at the level at which sexuality controls. Family controls at the level of inheritance, training, tradition. Sexuality controls at the level of the genes, and it is no wonder that the arc of the moral universe, as Dr King says, bends toward justice. In the long run, the genes and all that they control, are going to win out. The genes are going to demand what they demand. Mankind will be free. And all that gets in the way of the genes will be discarded. The actions that make man unfree will be abandoned. This does not mean that we, by the end, will become creatures only of our genes, automatons, acting without thinking and without volition. But it does mean that the freedom our genes demand must be unfettered.

4

When I came to address the question of how to put the novel together, I thought I wanted to resist the tendency to make coming out the goal of the narrator's life. The reader would get anxious or impatient if "coming out" were the goal. Particularly if "coming out" were tardy or slow-in-coming. So I started *Race Point Light* in Provincetown, with four or five pages on Fair Shaw as a gay man with his partner, late in his life. In this beginning, Fair Shaw talks about the sea and the shore and AIDS and their connection with memory. He mentions their host for the weekend, whose condo walls are covered with framed snapshots of beautiful men lying on the beaches of Provincetown.

I proposed to follow this opening with small snapshots of the narrator's own memory—short paragraphs of beautiful men from his childhood and youth and young adulthood. These had no connection to one another, but they introduced the idea of the sea and the shore and the erotic memory and, I hoped, showed where the novel was going to go, even if it didn't tell how it was going to get there. The novel was going to start where it started—on the beach in Provincetown—and then at the end of the novel arrive back where it had begun, on the beach at Provincetown. And the point of the novel was not to answer the question, *What happens next?* but to ask the question, *What happens to get him from the beach in Provincetown through 60 years finally to the beach again in Provincetown?* The question of the novel was, then, *How did he get here? What adventures did he have getting here?*

Since I was so late dealing with my birth family, since I was so hesitant to bring about a final rupture with them, and since a final rupture with them was so necessary to confronting any of the other issues in front of me, and since I couldn't respect myself as a gay man as long as I respected them, it seemed as if I couldn't proceed without breaking up my birth family. I resisted for years. In *Race Point Light*, it happens at the same time, very late in the novel, as Fair Shaw is visiting the hospital of a man who has AIDS. Something snaps in him and the connection is broken. The break is so savage and so absolute—it happened over a payphone while Shaw was standing on the sidewalk outside the hospital—that there is no way it can be reconnected. Shaw knows it can only be restarted, completely, from the beginning. And that was not going to happen.

I hoped to encourage the reader to understand that I knew where I was going, that there was no suspense in this tale except insofar as *how* was the suspenseful question.

5

Pretty quickly I understood that *Race Point Light* would be made up of six "parts," and that each part would be located in a specific place. Columbia, South Carolina, the US Army in Yakima, Washington (as well as Columbia, South Carolina, and

Vanderbilt University in Nashville, Tennessee), Ann Arbor, Michigan, the University of Maine in Orono, Maine, and then the last two in Boston, Massachusetts. These were roughly the five "places" of my life stretched out to six. I could easily see that each of these "parts" could focus on periods of my life— my childhood and education, my young adulthood, my military service, my heterosexual marriage, my alcoholism, and my experience of the AIDS epidemic and of gay activism—to counter the deadening effect of one-thing-after-another. I wanted to surprise the reader at each new "part." The reader would turn the page and would not find what he or she expected. For example, instead of the hedonism which might have been expected after the narrator's coming out, the reader found himself reading about an AA meeting and AIDS. This happens in big and small ways all the way through the book.

Fair Shaw has gotten his doctorate at the end of Part 2, and the reader's attention then is given over to the seeming collapse of western culture at the beginning of Part 3. This was not merely a narrative device. It had come to seem to me that we are constantly surprised by our lives, and that it is the narrative that says nothing changes that is the real "fictional" device.

I was careful with smaller units, too. I was very careful about the order in which I dealt with the material in Part 1. In developing the character of Fair Shaw, I knew that I had to confront his family's alcoholism, all the members of his family who were alcoholics, his family's history in South Carolina, his class, his education, his gender expression, his sexuality, among other things. In confronting these issues, I had to decide how to present them to the reader, when to present them to the reader, the order in which they are presented. I made lists, rearranged the lists, experimented with text, cut, pasted, threw stuff away, and a lot more, and then came up with what the text is now. My goal was always to make a very good novel about a gay man who was going through his teenage years in the nineteen-fifties which then affected all his later life. In other words, my goal was to make a very good novel about a gay man who, from his earliest childhood to the very verge of old age, knows he has to fight back.

6

Fair Shaw spent much of his early life in an academic setting, either in school or teaching. Eventually he left the academic world for the freedom of Boston during AIDS. He took with him a lot of what he had learned over the years. For example, when he was writing, and when he was starting a new chapter, he might think of the way Shakespeare started *King Lear*:

> *Enter Kent, Gloucester, and Edmund*
> Kent: I thought the King had more affected the Duke of Albany than Cornwall.
> Gloucester: It did always seem so to us; but now, in the division of the kingdom, it appears not which of the dukes he values most, for equalities are so weighed that curiosity in neither can make choice of either's moiety.
> Kent: Is not this your son, my lord?
> Gloucester: His breeding, sir, hath been at my charge. I have so often blushed to acknowledge him that now I am brazed to it. [1,1,1-11]

Thus begins *King Lear,* one of the great plays in any language, with a jocular exchange between gentlemen about a boy conceived out of wedlock. But he shows the novice writer something important. The way to get into the first great scene of the play—the division of the kingdom—he has two characters of secondary importance enter and set the scene, talking about something else entirely, apparently merely to accustom the audience to the scene and to them and to what is about to happen. To know that a play can be begun this way is invaluable. And the nonsense about the parentage of Edmund is, it turns out, not nonsense. For Kent and Gloucester are talking about parentage and parenting and love between a father and his sons, and those are the subjects of the play, except it is the king and his daughters.

As for my subject, I learned nothing, or little, during school except how good it felt. In the 1950s and 1960s, the academic world was hardly more enlightened than the rest of our culture on issues around homosexuality. And when it came time for Fair Shaw to leave teaching, the homophobia of his fellow teachers was a significant part of his reason for leaving.

7

The difficulty with much of this is that there was much about the nineteen-fifties which was hidden. It was the Cold War, and much of what was shaping the culture during the period was led by the CIA and other governmental bodies who were manipulating society to their own ends. This is not to say that all secret government activities during the Cold War were wrong and corrupted our society. What I do know is that secret government activity by the CIA which sought to manipulate society's expression of gender or society's attitude toward sexuality and sought to prevent homosexuality from being accepted into mainstream American society was wrong, anti-American, un-Constitutional, and bad for America.

The CIA worked through a dummy organization called The Congress for Cultural Freedom (CCF). With CIA money it made an impression on American culture after the war. A mechanism for spreading money around the culture, it awarded prizes and fellowships, founded organizations, all to support the organizations and writers and artists, dancers, actors, who were willing to support the goals of the CCF, which were supporting high culture generally and a certain kind of literature. The college I started in, in Tennessee, published the *Sewanee Review*, one of the literary journals given money by the CCF and consequently by the CIA. And it was evidently a school devoted to the concept of high culture. "High culture" meant the kind of visual art that was fashionable in New York after the war. It meant Jackson Pollack and Adolph Gottlieb and the abstract expressionists, among other things. In literary terms, it meant T.S.Eliot, the New Criticism and the kinds of work published in the little magazines—*Kenyon Review, Sewanee Review, Poetry, Partisan Review, Hudson Review, Journal of the History of Ideas*, and *Daedalus*, all of which got money from the CCF and consequently from the CIA. The amounts of money were small. The CCF agreed to buy, for example, one thousand copies of an issue of the *Sewanee Review*—that is, to pay the *Review* a stipend in the amount of the cost of one thousand copies of the Review. Since it was a quarterly, the CCF agreed to pay this stipend four times a year. George Kennan, architect of the American post war foreign policy, was also "the architect of the policy of harnessing culture to the political imperatives of the Cold War." (Saunders, p. 246) To put this into perspective, the *Sewanee Review* only sold about 2500 copies per issue, and the CIA purchase only increased this figure by 1000. Even 3500 copies in the issue is a minuscule number when compared to the press run of *The New Yorker*, for example, even in 1957. Yet, these little magazines, most of them, led the field. They set the standards for the rest of the literary magazines. They were well edited and set a very high bar for high quality literature. And their relatively few copies went to the most important 2500 addresses in the humanities in America. All the top libraries, most of the top people in the universities, publishing, and book sales. The fact that they were taking money from the CIA in order to encourage bigotry against LGBTQ American citizens was not disclosed.

The difficulty with writing about all this is having to accept the fact that most people in America in the 1950s didn't know they were being manipulated by the government and therefore didn't see the government as the enemy. Fair Shaw's maternal family simply took what the government said as the truth, and Fair Shaw's college professors had simply taken on good faith what the editors who ran the literary journal published by the university said about sexuality. The effect of this on a particular student like Fair Shaw, who was gay, was incalculable and, in fact, was not calculated until fifty years later, with the publication of books like Frances Stoner Saunders, *The Cultural Cold War: The CIA in the World of Arts and Letters. New York: New Press, 2001.* As I have written, much literature has been lost to us because of these "Cold War intellectuals."

The inability of a gay man to marry his lover was only one of the major disabilities experienced by LGBTQ persons in this period. Another was the danger of the sodomy laws, which made it a crime for men to have sex with one another. The desire of a young guy who wanted to write but was thwarted by *Stories with a homosexual theme are not accepted* was another.

And in the case of my narrator, Fair Shaw, it is not certain which of these three disabilities imposed by the Government of the United States of America was the more damaging to LGBTQ persons. Even if few people were charged under the sodomy laws, students across the country were expelled from schools because someone said they were homosexuals. They were dropped from the Boy Scouts, or some other organization. It was in the air. Homosexuality is not a good thing to have.

8

In considering the kind of art that is *Race Point Light*, it is important to remember that, during the time of *Race Point Light*, that is, during the time period 1945-2005, modernist literature had already been established in America for twenty years. The whole satchel full of modernist innovations introduced by William Faulkner and William Carlos Williams and others, and by the little magazines. By the time *Race Point Light* was written, all the big anti-censorship court cases had already been decided in our favor. People were accustomed to reading big novels by William Gaddis, Thomas Pynchon, and others, in which the rules of composition were broken and which addressed giant social and political themes. There was nothing about either *Ceremonies* or *Race Point Light* that made them technically difficult for the reader. That bar had already been set with James Joyce's *Ulysses*, and *Finnegan's Wake*. But *Race Point Light* is different in that it takes a markedly different approach to the question of what is an LGBTQ life.

As I have said, the tradition in US publishing has been to see LGBTQ lives as consisting of two events—falling in love and coming out. It is only very recently that the publishing industry—some small segment of it—has come to see that on all the questions about LGBTQ life, there need be no "other side" provided. The writer does not have to present gay life as a subject to be argued over between "sides." The lives of gay people can be presented on their own terms, and it is expected that readers will accept them. One of the first readers of *Ceremonies,* who turned *Ceremonies* down for publication, complained that I had not included any straight characters. "So, you see," he said, "you have only given us one side of the argument." There is no argument. *Ceremonies* is a novel about grief—among other things—and my job as a writer was to write about grief and not about some bizarre argument over whether it was a good thing to do to murder a gay kid.

Fiction is a temporal art—a reader experiences fiction one word at a time, one word after another, that is, in time—and the natural subject of fiction is an object moving through time. This is the plot. But this temporal quality of fiction, which is derived from the artist's medium, is limiting, and sometimes a writer wants to create something that gives the effect of a piece of sculpture rather than a piece of fiction made of words, put down on a page one after another. What might structure a lengthy piece of fiction is an image, say, of the ocean at Race Point, the moon, the stars, the various perspectives, the various objects in sight, the various things we can see—beginning with the wall of snapshots in our host's condo all of men's sexy bodies—and feel. He's thinking of the dead at this moment. It is possible that the one-bit-at-a-time process is actually the one-detail-at-a-time on a wall of canvas, and that we are meant to remember every detail at the conclusion of the process. As you prepare to close the book, what you have is less *The End,* than the artist's-name-and-the-year: *Dwight Cathcart, 2007,* signaling that the work of pictorial art is done. It is probably true that *Race Point Light* is less like *War and Peace* than it is like *Guernica.*

August 5, 2018

Earthrise 9

Adam in the Morning

At one in the morning, 28 June 1969, the New York policemen from the 6th Precinct, led by Deputy Inspector Seymour Pine, raided the Stonewall Inn, a gay bar, on Christopher Street in the West Village in New York. This was normal. The cops had raided the same bar earlier that week, and they had raided three other bars in the weeks before. What was unusual that night was that, when the customers were herded out of the bar, instead of going submissively, they rioted. Before the night was over, there were several thousand on the street, and the next night there were twice that many. The cops lost control of the streets both nights. Then, four nights later, when the Village Voice misrepresented the riots, reporting that it was merely "fag follies," they rioted again.

Many of these facts about the riots are drawn from David Carter's book *Stonewall: The Riots and Sparked the Gay Revolution*. I used his book as the framework for my treatment of the riots in *Adam in the Morning*. It is a fine book. Other sources are listed in the text.

1

The first questions these facts raise are: *Why did LGBTQ people get so pissed*, when they hadn't gotten pissed before? It is possible that LGBTQ people had seen African-Americans demonstrating in the street for years—at least ten whole years—against the whole racist establishment, and it didn't seem to matter how effective African-Americans and their demonstrations in the street were or weren't, they got to express their anger. They were doing *something*. Now here the cops were dragging gay people off to jail who had done nothing but buy a drink. I think it swept the crowd that gay people had to follow the lead of black people. It was the *sixties* for God's sake. Inspector Pine and the Sixth Precinct cops had driven LGBTQ people to the point where they no longer cared who they offended or what they would do in return, or how much it hurt. They had turned the LGBTQ people into rioters.

Someone yelled something to the crowd when a woman was being beaten by the cops. *Help her!* is thought to be the first rebellious shout from the crowd, and then, since the abuse went on, the responses got bigger and louder and harder. Someone, frustrated at his or her inability to respond effectively, picked up a rock and threw it, and everybody saw that and looked around for rocks for themselves. Then the air was full of flying rocks and cans, all heading toward the cops around the door of the Stonewall Inn. That was when the riots were full on.

Something like this happened nationally. LGBTQ people had watched and participated in the civil rights movement while being abused themselves. Their anger at their own abuse was submerged beneath all the powers of the culture which were arrayed against them—the military, the State Department, the "helping" professions, the education establishment, which, at that time was being encouraged by the CIA to limit the participation of gay people in the culture, in sports, both collegiate and professional, and everywhere else in the culture.

It gradually came on some of them—LGBTQ persons—that they were an abused, discriminated-against minority just like blacks and women, and that the best response was to fight back. The culture assumes that gay people *ought to be stigmatized*, and the cops seemed to know that it is always gratifying to have someone less worthy than yourself to abuse.

Just as the Stonewall Riots started when someone shouted "Help her!" it was the Stonewall Riots themselves that seem to have set off the national gay liberation movement. The LGBTQ community, having watched and in many cases participated in the Civil Rights riots and demonstrations, was ready. It was also true that reaching the boiling point happened differently in different parts of the country, so that at the moment the LGBTQ community burst forth into riots in New York, there were other places that were on their own time schedule. In parts of the South it didn't happen for years.

It happened in New York on the early morning of June 28,1969, and the feeling, afterward, was that everything had changed. It certainly changed my life. I was living in the Midwest at the time. I realized that there was another option for a gay man, aside from marriage to a woman or a life in the shadows. Out and proud. And fighting back. And the question for me became *How long am I going to stay in my marriage to a woman? How long am I going to allow this stigma to be imposed on me?*

Years later, when I was thinking about all this, I wondered what had happened to all of us. We lived in a world where the people had been divided between men and women, and between those who desired to have sex with their own gender and those who desired to have sex with the opposite gender. By and large, these boundaries remained rigidly enforced; and therefore in many places, it was as difficult to be gay after Stonewall as it had been before Stonewall. Even as the social norms loosened up, that is, even as LGBTQ achieved more freedoms, gay people still held to the rigid demarcation between men and women and between gay and straight. You needed to be a women or a man—they wanted us to make up our minds—among most gay people and most straight people. It was a matter of pride among most people that one was able to say, *I've always fucked the opposite sex*, or *I have never fucked the opposite sex*. For most of my life, it has never been OK to say, *I don't know why it matters*.

Since it has been my experience that people do usually want the rest of us to choose, I wondered what happened to the liberation that Stonewall was supposed to bring. It was out of this quandary that the seed grew into *Adam in the Morning*. During the three nights of rioting, although everybody had the sense that everything had changed, you look at the issue of gender, and it is still clear after the riots that there are two genders, as there were before. It took another fifty years to get beyond that, and we're still struggling. And most people in the gay community still speak of gay and straight and even think that way while they have in their group of friends men and women who have been married and who have children and have had available to them Martin Duberman's *Stonewall*, and Alfred Kinsey's *Sexual Behavior of the Human Male* and its statistics, and who could know, if they wanted to, that there is not any clear division between gay and straight.

> 30% of all males have at least incidental
> homosexual experience or reactions (i.e. rate 1
> to 6 [on Kinsey's seven-point scale]) over at
> least a three-years period between the ages of 16

and 55. This accounts for one male out of every
three in the population who is past the early
years of adolescence (Table 150, Figure 168).
Kinsey, p. 650.

What happened at Stonewall that allowed it to go so far—
but not far enough? I was sitting in the swing on my daughter's
front porch on one night in 2007 and thought of people. I had
already written *Ceremonies, Winter Rain,* and *Race Point
Light,* and I thought I now wanted to write about men who had
already, even in June 28, 1969, moved beyond the coming out
issue. They were out and waiting for the next big thing. I knew
there were such men among the rioters at Stonewall from
having read David Carter's book, *Stonewall* (Chapters Three,
"On the Street," *passim* and Chapter Four,"The Stonewall Inn,"
passim), and other books about New York gay men. I thought it
would be important to explore how they responded to the riots.

Since I knew that the dominant image of the rioters was of
street people—that is, mostly homeless teenagers—I knew that
I needed source material for my guys. The rioters had not all
been Puerto Rican drag queens.

There were some lesbians, hustlers, married
people, single people, some transvestites, but
not too many. It was the heart and soul of the
Village because it had every kind of person
there. Carter, p. 67.

In writing the book, I felt an obligation to base a
description of a character on some person who had been
described in one of the histories of the Stonewall Riots. For
example, height. There seems to be an agreement that the
fiercest fighters were the street people, which implies shorter

people. Four of my characters, on the other hand, are grown men, six feet two inches tall. They are all based on a man named David Van Ronk, who was six feet five inches and apparently one of the first persons to be arrested in the riots. Von Ronk was straight and had come from a restaurant nearby to check out the scene. Having seen as much as he wanted to see, he turned to leave just as Deputy Inspector Pine and two other policemen pulled him off his feet and attempted to handcuff him (*Adam in the Morning*, p. 155-157). While many of the younger men or boys might have slender boyish bodytypes, at least some of the older ones had fully-grown and developed bodies.

The question of what a homosexual looks like occupies many more people than merely writers. John O'Brien was a college-aged member of the Young Socialist Alliance in New York. But he had been called in by the board of the YSA, in Carter's words,

> who were reluctant to believe that he was homosexual: not only was he a hard-working party member, but his very masculine demeanor —including a very muscular physique—did not fit the gay stereotype. He also knew he could deny the accusation and they would believe him and the matter would be forgotten. But for O'Brien this was the moment of truth. He decided not to compromise his integrity and was summarily thrown out. Carter, p. 120.

There were all body types at Stonewall, and, as a writer, I could choose among them any physical appearance that answered the needs I had while I was writing *Adam in the*

Morning. But it seemed to me that what I could not, as a writer about Stonewall, choose a style for a gay character or a body type and write as if that were the only style and body type on Christopher Street that night. As long as I acknowledged that there were many styles and body types participating in the riots, then I would be free to choose a limited number for my characters. I was limited only by my inability to give a body-type to a character who performed one of the significant acts of the riots. We don't know who threw the first brick or if there was a first brick, and the details of the riots remain hazy. As we saw from the release of the movie *Stonewall* by Roland Emmerich, people get attached to the idea, for example, that there was a person who threw the first brick in the riots and to there being one person who threw that first brick. They naturally want, I think, to give due attention to the race of the person among the fighters at the riots. In *Adam in the Morning* I stayed away from designating a person to throw the first rock or the first brick. I didn't know any more than anyone else knew who it was, in the first place, and this was not the story I was telling.

Another issue was *Would they fight?* Were these people politicized enough to actually take up arms against a sea of troubles that beset them? One of the first arrested was the musician Dave Van Ronk, the one who was straight and six feet five inches tall. It took three cops to handcuff Van Ronk. Much of the popular conception of the rioters had to do with gender expression—they were at the extremes of masculinity or of femininity. The issue of gender has always run through the Stonewall Riots.

Only men were thought to be fighters. The police felt they could treat LGBTQ people anyway they wanted because gay people weren't ever male enough to fight back. Cops could raid gay bars as often as they wanted because it was just easier to beat up gay people than "real" men.

The LGBTQ guys felt that this was at the root of the thousands-of-years-long oppression of LGBTQ people. And what was so shocking about the Stonewall Riots was that the rioters turned all that around. Fighting against the toughest cops in New York—the Tactical Police Force—they won. Drag Queens, some of whom were slender effeminate guys wearing dresses and makeup, along with many more-conventional males—tall men like 6'5" Dave Van Ronk, and "muscular physique" John O'Brien—all together won the riots.

Everyone understood that the goal was to take away the street from the cops, and if they could do that, they would win. They managed that for three nights, fighting against New York's finest riot troops, who never brought out their guns. They had brought out their guns against black citizens all across America, but they weren't going to bring out their biggest guns against American citizens who were largely white. I didn't know whether this was so, but it seemed so. We never were told whether they were given orders not to fire on us.

The answer to the question, *why did the rioters go so far, but not far enough?* seems unanswerable. Perhaps they were unable to see how *their own behavior* might be the cultural standard for the future for all people.

3

Bo Ravich is the narrator of *Adam in the Morning* and the guy that the rest of the characters gather around. He is about 30, he has a good relationship with both of his parents, and always has had. He loves them. He came out to them when he was 16. Bo is white, and his first boyfriend was African-American. His parents knew and were welcoming. He went to public schools in Houston, then to Oberlin and finally, for an MA, to the University of Chicago. He studied history and politics, and wrote his MA thesis on a nineteenth century anarchist named Alexander Beekman. Bo has a magnetic personality and attracts people. Since college he has done community organizing. He picked up carpentering along the way and became good at it in Alabama, when he was doing voter registration. Bo is a stage carpenter in a repertory company production of *The Tempest*. A nameless man after the second riot says to him, "Everybody knows who Bo Ravich is." One of Bo's closest friends is the 15 year-old girl taken in by Bo and his partner, Andrew. She is named Mitzi, and she is said to be tough and pretty when she gets her act together. When she doesn't, she's just tough. At the beginning she tries to steal Bo's wallet, now she comes and sleeps on the sofa every now and then. She tells Bo and the others to leave their wallets— except for one piece of ID—at home before they go to the second day's riot. Bo thinks ahead, making plans about their lives, and it's his apartment that they come back to every morning after the fighting.

It was important to me, in the course of writing my novel, that the novel be a realistic one, that it answer the question *How is it for you there?* in a real way to the reader and be convincing to that reader, convincing him or her that this set of riots in these days in the New York we know really could have been this way. I wrote the book as a novel, rather than as a history, because I didn't want to say, *this is the way it was for gay people there at that moment.* I am not sure that absolute truth can be expressed about human behavior, beyond a listing of certain facts. I wanted freedom to explore ideas and feelings behind the riots rather than the facts of the riots themselves. This required that I propose characteristics for each of my characters—give them a context—which were grounded in the

historic facts of the riots and which didn't distort the meaning
of the riots, but which explored the meaning of those facts, in
the way of all novels.

My character, Bo, came from a background which exists in
America and which was described for me by a person I have
known for almost fifty years. This person is white and during
her childhood and young adulthood, her parents, who were also
white, were on the faculty of an historically black college in the
South. She told me of going to Oberlin and of knowing about a
"Men's Co-op," which was composed of half straight men and
half gay men. I thought the presentation of the Stonewall Riots
in *Adam in the Morning* would be better grounded if the reader
knew that some of its characters had come from accommodations with Jim Crow made over decades by American citizens.
America is not composed of two kinds of people—progressive
and conservative—it is a kaleidoscope of people, and the shift
from conservative to something else may happen as one
crosses the street onto the campus of the local university or into
a diner. The shift may also happen as one moves from one part
of one's brain to another—one may be conflicted. These are
more telling, more interesting facts about Bo than if I were to
write, "Bo's parents are progressive." One is always, to some
extent, at war, not merely with the Tactical Police Force but
with parts of oneself, but it is very interesting that this war is
with the culture and, like all wars, causes pain.

Andrew is Bo's boyfriend. Andrew is based on a character
Carter describes. He is separated from his parents because,
when he was in college, his parents didn't want a gay son
around anymore. They offered to send him to Europe for a year
if he would give up "this thing you are so addicted to," but he
refused. He was already at Columbia, and was a member of the
first gay student organization in America, The Student

Homophile League. With the support of his dean, and with loans and scholarships, he remained a student at Columbia until graduation. His parents don't have anything to do with him. He's a waiter, and he writes for the *RAT*, the SDS paper, the *East Village Other,* the *Guardian*, the *Queen's Quarterly, Gay Power,* and *Screw* and other counter-culture rags in New York and elsewhere on the East Coast. Bo says he is brilliant. Like Bo, Andrew's life is a history of accommodation to abuse. He got an education largely before his parents decided to crack the whip, and then he learned to support himself and finish his education by waiting tables, all the while plotting revolution. His first response to the riots was to start a newspaper. As Bo says, it is his anger at his parents that drives him. The conflict between Andrew and his parents is a relationship which many novels have been written about, *Tom Jones*, for an early example, proving that a novel can be driven by a conflict over political points of view between characters tied together by blood. It almost is in *Cat on a Hot Tin Roof.* Bo says that Andrew is "the most dispossessed of the four of us," and "When Andrew wades into the battle on Christopher Street, he carries all these things on his back, this anger and hurt." When I was writing this book, I wanted to show how, exactly how, a political conflict can lead to intensely personal hurt. There you have it.

Another person in that repertory company is Joseph, an actor, who shows up in Part 1 of the novel at the first riot and goes home with the others after the fighting is over for eggs and bacon and talk and sex. Bo and Andrew like him, and he becomes part of the gang. He's had experience in voter registration in Mississippi—Bo was also there—and he had experience in urban riots in Watts. He has a single mother, who raised him, and with whom he has a good, warm relationship. She understood why he needed to go to Mississippi for

Freedom Summer and didn't guilt-trip him. She's proud of him. He and Mitzi know more about street fighting than anybody else, and Mitzi trusts him more than the others, although she doesn't understand acting. *How do you make a living pretending to be somebody else?*

Joseph comes from families of black people who are Caribbean-Americans—the French West Indies. When writing about him, I wanted to know more about the way black people came to America and found that the black families from the French West Indies came to Miami and then to New Orleans. They didn't get to Los Angeles until about 1941. Joseph was two or three years old.

Joseph is the most politically sophisticated of the group. He's up on black political theory. He points out that a good case can be made that black people should adopt a policy of separatism. Black leaders like Huey Newton and Eldridge Cleaver and Malcolm X had been saying just prior to June 28, 1969, that black people should separate themselves from white people for their better development. This point is discussed, seriously, and what is also discussed is its effect on the growing relationship between Joseph, who is black, and Bo and Andrew, who are white, and, of course, its implications for the relationship between LGBTQ persons and the straight people in America.

What was interesting to me about these discussions was the fact that you don't often read gay novels which address this kind of issue, where a political situation causes a character deep pain. The "political situation" arising out of communal or societal determinations as well as state or federal legal determinations cause problems for the character. Novels have, more generally, arisen out of a more personal conflict. Joseph says he is falling in love with Bo and Andrew, and they discuss moving in together, and then, on Tuesday night, he says *We need to discuss this more thoroughly.* Then he says, *I am black, and you are white, and we have not discussed enough what that means.* Now this is the kind of conflict that I am addressing here, which LGBTQ literature, in particular, has not addressed.

This is not caused by some moral failing by any of the characters, nor, for that matter, by many gay authors. Nor is it caused by personal quirks conveyed by any of them. *I don't choose men very well.* It is caused by a political and societal requirement placed on humans—I speak here of regulations like those that prevent marriage among same sex persons or adoption—that humans, by nature, don't submit to comfortably and do submit to differently. Some people adjust to these requirements better than others, some people don't notice them, some make interesting accommodations, and some commit suicide.

The root cause of the way these people live their lives is that they live in a culture that makes requirements of them that they are not naturally responsive to. It is not a case, when you are growing up, that you learn you must work hard to succeed in life. It is not even a case that you learn you must control to some degree your sex drive. Our culture has developed marriage or living together or casual sex in response to those needs. But if my culture attempts to control my sex, it is attempting to control something that arises ultimately out of my genes and in its development passes through deep parts of my brain. The culture is attempting to control parts of a human that simply cannot be controlled and are beyond choice. I think this is the reason so many countries have imposed capital punishment—execution—on homosexuals. They can't control homosexuality in any other way than by cutting off our heads or burning us alive or, lately, throwing us off the roofs of buildings. They can't make them stop. When I was growing up in the South, I learned that my culture was racist, and, later, homophobic, and instead of stopping my actions, which were offensive to them, I moved, then I moved again, and finally I left my profession, divorced my wife, and moved again. There aren't many novels about men in that situation. But there are many hundreds of thousands of men in that situation.

Mitzi is a fifteen-year-old street kid, homeless, and no education. She doesn't have the advantages the three men in the group have, the principal one being education. Whatever crimes Mitzi commits, and she commits some crime about every twenty minutes when she's on the street, they are overwhelmed by the crimes her society commits against her. She was thrown out on the street when she was thirteen, and she was provided with no support from the city, state, or federal governments thereafter. When Bo and Andrew offer to buy her a hamburger after she tries to steal Bo's wallet, she is deeply suspicious, thinking they are plainclothes cops. Every time they do anything for her, she wants to know what they want for it. Her most significant quality is her bravery, which shades over into bravado at times. She is heard saying, "I don't take shit from nobody."

"I think," Mitzi says at another point, "every time I go on the street I'm giving the finger to everybody in power, and I know that, and I think they know that too." *Adam in the Morning*, p. 93.

Sometimes the political conflict at the heart of a novel is not so much a struggle as it is a refusal to bend, and that is Mitzi's way. Bo says of her,

> The truth is, at fifteen, she has to take shit from
> a lot of people, because that's the way things are
> set up. It's the system, is what people say. It's
> illegal for her to be on the street the way she is,
> and the cops can sweep her up and charge her

with any number of crimes—with loitering, with panhandling, with creating a public nuisance, with prostitution, with vagrancy, with having homosexual sex, with wearing clothes that the arresting officer can say are not appropriate to her gender—and throw her into juvenile detention where she'll be held until the criminal justice system is ready to send her to serious incarceration, and to do this so often that she will accumulate a long list of convictions so that each new sentencing will be of a repeat offender. She will end up spending the rest of her life trapped in the criminal justice system. It's a trap she's in and can almost not get out of, and all of this over gender violations so innocuous that, left alone, they would not damage a fly. It is important to remember that the folks charged with her care—her parents—threw her out on the street when she was thirteen. While murders go unsolved and public funds are embezzled and public officers are bribed—and the Constitution deeply violated by the highest officials in the nation—Mitzi and her brothers and sisters are tracked down in the public street by all the armed might of the city. Our culture never gave Mitzi much to begin with, and then it took away what it gave, and then it hounds her for not having what it's taken away. And in the end, the newspapers call her and Violet and all their brothers and sisters the "dregs of the city." *Adam in the Morning*, p. 204.

Saturday night, the four of them are walking up Christopher Street toward 7th Avenue, looking for the riots. They had been talking about the street kids, and their bravery on the street. It seems, at the end of the novel, that Mitzi changes less than anybody else. It may be at her age and in her condition, that she had to be more rigid than the others just to survive. The others were stronger and more able to fight. It may be that her last chance to change—her Stonewall—was on her thirteenth birthday, so she had already made the changes she needed to make. She had learned what the world was like and what she had to do to live in it.

4

Sometimes I think that *Adam in the Morning* comes closer to my conception of a political novel than anything else I have written. The obstacles were clear, the goal was clear, and the difficulties the various people had with doing what they had to do were also clear. The Stonewall Riots are the iconic event in the history of gay liberation, even if there are other events that should be in that place. And so far as I know there has never been a novel about it. Our writers could focus on these great moments—not necessarily the best known, for I include here the narratives of *Ceremonies* and *of Race Point Light*—and write about how they affected our people and how our people affected them. The people in these novels, when they define their opponents, don't go far enough beyond the phrase "the system." Ruminating before he leaves the theatre to stumble into the riot the middle of the night Friday, Bo thinks this:

> There's a reason Negroes in America are poor and
> badly educated and have been for hundreds of
> years. There's a reason that even Negroes in the

North all live in ghettos. A class of people—that is, white men—benefits from keeping Negroes off the voter rolls and poor and down trodden. It is not merely that white men get rich off the backs of poor Negroes, although that's true of some of them. It is that keeping Negroes down and keeping poor people down enable rich white men to decide how our cities are going to look and what countries we are going to attack and what ones are going to be our allies and to set up the tax laws and the welfare laws the way they find most beneficial to them, and enable white men to decide what books are going to be published on what subjects and enable white men to write the history books with the great narrative of the last 350 years in America and to apportion responsibility and blame in a way that is beneficial to them. One of the things the system accomplishes is that it enables those in power to escape responsibility and to blame others for their crimes and failures. *Adam in the Morning,* p. 4-5.

Bo gets it. It's a "system" that's screwing everything up, and the guys, including Mitzi, seem to understand that, but they drop back and don't go far enough. In *Adam in the Morning*, I went as far as the historical record allowed me to go. I wanted this novel to be about the real details of this real event, and I didn't want to give the characters information that was not generally available until later. It is only now, in 2018, that the youngest generation among us are demanding real changes to "the system, " and our society is finally realizing and becoming comfortable with the fact that our society has many more genders than two and many more problems than whether to give LGB persons their rights—and who else to give their right to. Our society will come to see problems we didn't see before, writers will write about those problems when they didn't before, publishers will publish, and booksellers will sell those books, and readers will buy and read them, opening up another vast world of subjects that require the close attention of the whole publishing industry, including the attention of publishers' to ebooks and to POD books. A vast world of serious problems in the culture is going to need solving to bring them in line with the reality of our lives. This is the movement that will bring us all closer to the success that I mentioned at the beginning of this essay. It will immeasurably enrich our literature, and consequently leave behind us a more complete record of our lives.

August 28, 2018

Earthrise10

Winter Rain

1

I set out to write a gay novel about alcoholism, and when I completed it and then couldn't get it published, I put it in a box on the floor at the back of my closet. It eventually was moved to my first computer, and then moved from computer to computer. The editor who had rejected it had suggested that I try other publishers—these decisions were inevitably subjective, he said—but I was discouraged by the fact that two of my books had already been rejected, so I never sent it out again. It stayed on the floor of my closet and on my computer while I wrote *Race Point Light* and *Adam in the Morning,* and while I published *Ceremonies*, and *Race Point Light* and *Adam in the Morning.* Finally, after the three books were published as ebooks and as print-on-demand books, my daughter asked me what I had done with *Winter Rain*, which she had read shortly after I completed it. So, 28 years after I had written it, I read it again. When I wrote it, I was intent on capturing the sense of helplessness that often accompanies late-stage alcoholism. I had been frustrated by the inability of other recovering alcoholics to capture how it felt to be unable to stop drinking.

Around the time I was thinking about this book, I saw an article in the *Boston Globe* about a police car found on the street in a town north of Boston. Nearby was a body of a man who had been hit by a car. He was dead. Investigation showed that the man had been killed by the car. What was not clear was who had driven the car. He or she was not found, and there was no evidence linking the owner of the car to the car. This story ran for several days in the *Globe,* and I was struck by the horror of being the owner of the car—who was said to be a state policeman—and to have been too drunk to know whether he himself had driven his own car at that moment. In the following weeks, the state and the city police mounted intense investigations into the question of who had driven the car at the moment the car killed the man. There were no witnesses who could identify the driver, and the owner of the car was in blackout, apparently.

About the same time, psychologists and psychiatrists were leading patients to believe that symptoms could lead a therapist to determine whether a patient had been sexually abused. I knew of people accused of sexual abuse who asked, *When was I supposed to have done this?* and were told, *I don't know. My therapist tells me that the way I am now indicates it did happen. I don't know when. I think it was when I knew you.* The man's symptoms added up to the hypothesis that he had been subject to sexual abuse by somebody, sometime, somewhere. And while charges were made and investigations mounted and lives ruined, some people realized that it was not provable and some therapists stopped countenancing a charge of sexual abuse against people on the basis of recovered memory.

In 1990, the AIDS crisis deepened. The heterosexual

community was beginning to see that anyone could be infected. At that point a relative told me that the ones she felt sorriest for were the innocent victims, the wives and children of the men who had had sex with other men and who were infected with HIV, and had then passed it on to their wives and children. This kind of stupidity and insensitivity was everywhere. Other factors made the situation worse. The decision not to push prevention strategies in the LGBTQ and black communities was largely made because the Roman Catholic church was against the use of condoms. The fewer people who used condoms, the more cases of AIDS there will be. I was about fifty when I was putting all this together in the novel that became *Winter Rain.* Nationally George H. W. Bush was being as stubborn as Ronald Reagan about LGBTQ issues, and internationally Bush was leading a coalition of nations who seemed to be determined to undo the delicate balance in the Mideast and bring war to the Persian Gulf. I had just completed *Ceremonies,* and I wanted to write a novel about one man and do it from the third person point-of-view. I wanted to get outside the protagonist as another way of getting at what was happening to him. I started with a man coming up out of the subway entrance—coming up out of the ground—running toward a hospital where his friend and former lover lay comatose with AIDS.

When this book was completed and submitted to publishers —in this case, it was Michael Dennehy and St. Martin's Press in New York—I had great hopes for a sale of the novel because I was sure the novel was a good one and because St. Martin's had the reputation of wanting to publish serious gay fiction. Also, Michael Dennehy was gay, and it would seem that, if Winter Rain were to get a positive reading, this would be it. I sent it off with great hopes. I was younger than I am now and naive.

Earthrise 10

It was rejected. Mr. Dennehy himself wrote the letter, telling me I was a good writer, but the people sitting around the conference table seemed unsure about what I was doing in *Winter Rain*. I was, they seemed to think, asking a great deal of the reader. And that was bad. I thought, Well, I was. I was asking my reader to put himself in the place of an LGBTQ man or woman from that period who was fighting the various storms that were hitting LGBTQ people. There is a man lying near death from AIDS—one of many persons with AIDS. There was a national debate going on over whether these people did it to themselves by engaging in unsafe sexual practices. At the same time there was virtually universal condemnation of the promiscuity of gay men, which some people said caused the AIDS case in the first instance. But I gave the reader no help in understanding whether this man deserves our sympathy—that is, whether he is a victim or whether he deserves what he's getting. To top it all off, the novel ends without telling the reader what caused this. Other things happen in *Winter Rain* that seem like random events but that seem to beg you to wonder *what caused this?* The editors at St. Martin's press rejected because there was too much bad luck striking its characters, too much coincidence. It moved too far from the Aristotelian yoking of character and circumstance. When tragedy arrives and the health of the community decays, people want to find the person responsible. People look for a personal character flaw in the leader, some failure to act quickly enough—He procrastinates. Or he is ambitious. Or jealous. Or *He ever but slenderly knew himself.* But the flaw in the answer is implicit in the question. There may not be a person who is responsible. It may be bad luck, it may be the way organizations or systems operate, it may be the way humans are: if you do this, others around you will do that, even if this is not only legal but natural.

2

Alec bursts in on us, coming up out of the ground as if he were rising from the dead, has a drink, and runs across the street to the hospital, where Amos is silent and still in his hospital room. Here begins the final judgment of Alec Argento.

The question that *Winter Rain* sets out to answer is *What did Alec Argento do?* We have seen him drinking. We know his son feels betrayed. We know he gives Amos a bed to die in. We know he got in a fight with his brother. He drives his father crazy. We know just about everything that he did for four or five days, and almost none of them reflect well on Alec. He was drinking too much to be responsible and on-time and steady.

The last pages of *Winter Rain* show how difficult it is to tell whether Lear was right when he said, "I am a man more sinned against than sinning." How can you judge what Lear says? Alec provided a communal space for his friends through these days, and then, when Amos is dying and the hospital had nothing left they could do for him, Alec provided him with a place to die. The question for me was, *How do I take a man who has done so much to hurt other people and write it so that he breaks my heart with his grief?* How do I write it—at least two men die violently, a marriage breaks up, two men who love one another split up, a father loses his son—so that it is possible that no one can find out who caused all this. *Who is guilty?*

There is no way to assign guilt to one person, but even if guilt can be assigned, it cannot be assigned to one person or even to several. *Who are the good people?* More pointedly, *who wins in this contest?* And before that, the question is, *Who's right?* And, of course, *how does one tell? Count votes? Count money? Count friends? Power? Count the number who*

99

are still alive? Is that what we're doing? Men used to do this differently from women, but I suspect the difference is getting less and less. What happens in this novel is that Alec Argento starts off, almost right away, battling something and, the reader fears, losing. But he isn't defeated, *he loses.* Then we discover that that was only one race. He was also running another race, difference shows, different terrain, and something is going wrong there, too. We gradually come to see that this guy is in conflict from every angle—it's coming at him from every direction, one of which is his father—and he's just not in good enough shape to win everywhere at once.

Often guilt can't be assigned. There is just no person who is guilty. Often it is hard to assign a cause of any kind. To answer the question, *Who was driving the car?* What causes a volcano? A hurricane, in which thousands die? The editor I sent this novel to, the head of St. Martin's Press, said that his staff, sitting around a conference table, concluded that I had just asked too much of my readers. I posed the possibility that my protagonist had killed a man, then I had withdrawn the possibility of finding out whether he had killed a man. That was true of killing the other man too, and it was true of the question of who passed HIV to whom, when the virus had invaded their relationship. It was also true of the armies who fought around the Gulf, but it was posed in a slightly different way. *Whose armies imposed the greatest carnage on the other?* Or *who caused the particular carnage that killed this man.* We are left with the man and his pain and with no way to tell whether he himself caused the pain. And as for the armies in the desert, Matthew Arnold said *they are ignorant and clash by night.* I think our tendency—that is, all of us, all the time—when things go wrong is to look for the person who caused it. *Ah-ha! You did this!* We can draw and quarter you and then things will be OK again. But sometimes that doesn't help.

Sometimes there are simply too many people who have failed, and in many cases, the damage is done and can't be undone and the damage is so immense, so all-encompassing, that it belittles the actions that caused it. We are in too much pain to stop and try to indict them and convict them.

3

When writers confront the issues of pain, death, defeat, they inevitably have to ask *why*. Pride used to lead to error and to violation of moral codes. What infected the nation was the violation of national moral codes by the king's hamartia. There was a solution to the infected nation, which was to kill the disobedient. There are other ancient sources. In *The Book of Job*, men, seeing the afflictions visited upon Job, ask him to curse God.

> Then the Lord answered Job out of the
> whirlwind, and said, Who is this that darkeneth
> counsel by words without knowledge? Gird up
> now thy loins like a man; for I will demand of
> thee, and answer thou me. Where wast thou
> when I laid the foundations of the earth? *Book
> of Job,* KJV, 38, 1-4

In the story of *Sodom and Gomorrah,* God sends angels to speak to Lot, for whole cities are supposedly to be destroyed for willfully violating God's will.

> And the men said unto Lot, Hast thou here any
> besides? son-in-law, and thy sons, and thy
> daughters, and whatsoever thou hast in the city,
> bring them out of this place: For we will

> destroy this place, because the cry of them is
> waxen great before the face of the Lord; and the
> Lord hath sent us to destroy it. And Lot went
> out, and spake unto his sons-in-law, who
> married his daughters, and said, Up, get you out
> of this place; for the Lord will destroy this city.
> But he seemed as one that mocked unto his sons
> in law. *Genesis,* KJV, 19, 12-14

This kind of clarity we don't see much of anymore. What we do see is something closer to the *Poetics* of Aristotle, where the failure is less in disobedience than in error. Hamartia, often used as a synonym for pride, can be seen also as a synonym for mistake or failure. Hamartia is a human aspect that is entirely within the human himself or herself. There is no divine entity involved in hamartia. What we are addressing here is the connection between pain and suffering, on the one hand, and its cause, on the other. What we are seeing is that connection as it developed over the most recent twenty-five hundred years of our Western culture.

A later illustration was the various plagues that swept Europe during the Middle Ages 1347-1351, killing between one-third and two-thirds of the population, or between 75 and 200 million people. As with *Job* and *Sodom and Gomorrah*, there were ritual references to "God" and references to the sins of the people, and connections between the sins causing the destruction and the need to placate an angry God, but several things continued—kings still died, ordinary people suffered and died, and people wanted relief from their pain and suffering. They gradually prayed to God less and less, but they had substitutes.

In our time, the Christian Right blames LGBTQ people for

national catastrophes. They are the ones who caused it all. Conservatives blame liberals. Republicans blame Democrats. White Americans blame Black Americans. But the trouble is, the pain goes on no matter who is blamed, no matter what the pain is—a war in Southeast Asia, in the Gulf States, the deaths of hundreds of thousands from AIDS, the deaths of persons by vigilante gangs, a man in his twenties with an assault weapon and the ability to get into a grammar school. The trouble with *We have to find who caused this* is that *this* in our time is so vast—during the initial bombing of the Gulf War, the one that starts on page one of *Winter Rain*, there were 156,143 people in the US dead of AIDS—that it was like charging an army with murder. The Gulf War, with which *Winter Rain* starts, started with an aerial bombardment on January 16, 1991. Iraqi military casualties are believed to range between 20,000 and 35,000 men, women, and children. Civilian casualties are approximately 3500 men, women, and children from bombing, and 100,000 men, women, and children from other causes. The US forces fatalities were 149 men and women, and a few fatalities among other causes. It was not like finding the man who killed the old lady down the street. The story of *Winter Rain* is the story of Alec Argento, who suffers, but who suffers from the same thing that is killing everybody north of the Missouri. Or everybody named Smith in the Manhattan phonebook. It is impossible to know who suffers hamartia. How many men and women. How many thousands. Millions. And whether that had anything at all to do with the pain.

In 1991, during the *Winter Rain* narrative, the CDC announced that 1,000,000 Americans were infected with HIV. WHO estimated that nearly 10 million people were infected with HIV worldwide, 206,563 cases of AIDS reported at that date and 156,143 deaths to Americans. Amos is one of them. I thought, when I first started thinking about this book, that it would be about alcoholism, but in the book I wrote, the alcoholic has a friend with AIDS, and then, I realized, the focus of the book inevitably shifted. And, in 2018, it was reported in the *Washington Post* that more than 300 Catholic priests across Pennsylvania sexually abused children over seven decades, protected by a hierarchy of church leaders who covered it up, according to a sweeping grand jury report released Tuesday. The investigation, one of the broadest inquiries into church sex abuse in U.S. history, identified 1,000 children who were victims, but reported that there probably are thousands more. Pope Francis, responding to the report of the grand jury in Pennsylvania, has this to say in the *Daily Wire*: Pope Francis implored the hierarchy of the Catholic Church to pray and resist the "Great Accuser," Satan, who seeks to expose sin in order to divide the faithful.

Well, no shit. The impulse to blame somebody seems to be universal and eternal. It may be that the impulse to blame oneself is the most universal of all. Pain seems universal and eternal. Lear knew this. Job is taught this. An argument can be made that tragedy was the most popular dramatic form during the Renaissance just because it recognizes the existence of pain and then assigns blame. Laertes says, as he dies, "The king, the king's to blame," [*Hamlet,* 5.2.320] People pay money to see other people suffer. Or to see the king suffer. But it may be that something else is going on. It may be that people pay money to see someone experience what they themselves experience many days of the week—that is, pain.

4

Every immigrant from south of the US border knows this. Every child sexually abused knows this, too. When Alec comes up out of the ground, his drink at the bar soothes him temporarily, and the visit to Amos's hospital room reminds us what the stakes are.

There is much pain in the world which does not derive its source from some cause, which is to say some choice which humans make. Earth was not perfectly made for us, and the conditions of our residence here include places which give intense and long-lasting pain. Disease. What is the cause of cancer? Medical science assumes that eventually they will find some gene which fails in its job and then we will be told, *We have found the cause of cancer.* But that is not so. The question which needs to be answered is, *Why is there a gene which can fail and cause cancer?* If you remove bigotry from the equation, a person is left with an Earth which contains HIV and its disease, AIDS, for no reason. To be clear: the overwhelming suffering of the LGBTQ community and of the communities of color in America is not caused by anything except a bacterium in the wrong place—or doctors have not yet found the right med yet. The world is full of dangerous things, and it is bad luck if you become infected. There is no way to control when medicine will develop a vaccine. Despite conspiracy theories about the CIA and HIV, nobody did anything to make that happen. The connection between disease and human agency has been largely broken. The result is that much of what we experience is the result of a host of choices a person has made throughout his or her life—not to smoke, to swim regularly, eat well—and also a result of an even larger host of things we can only suffer through or suffer until we die. In the end of course, no matter how healthy our choices, we die.

Consider also the condition of alcoholism. While scientists have searched for a cause of the disease, they have not found one, no choice which humans make which causes alcoholism or they have found so many as to be confusing and unhelpful. Some people, in one biological family, develop alcoholism and others, in the same family, don't. Why does one person drink and then stop drinking at a certain point, and another person similarly situated drinks and then is unable to stop drinking? While uncontrollable drinking seems to be a definition of alcoholism, and it seems true that it would be easy to reduce one's alcohol consumption, which would put the person in control of his health, still the question remains, *Why does this man drink uncontrollably and that one doesn't?* We seem to be able, with many people, to help a person stop drinking after he has become an alcoholic, but we are unable to prevent alcoholism entirely from occurring. We seem to be in the same place as with AIDS. A person's body for some unknown reason develops an uncontrollable desire to drink alcohol. Morality seems to have nothing to do with it. Character seems to have nothing to do with it. Reason seems to have nothing to do with it. Faith changes nothing. Alcoholism is a devastating disease and extremely painful, and people on Earth seem to be in the appalling position of being unable to protect themselves from it any more than they can protect themselves from AIDS. It is one of the dangers of being alive, and it is senseless pain.

5

It is unlikely that we are going to create a world without pain. And most of the time, the pain we experience is not so much pain caused by a single person—my landlord, for example, or Lee Harvey Oswald, or, for that matter, our current president— as pain we can't do anything about and have to live with. Alec Argento's life is like this. He is an alcoholic, Amos is almost dead from AIDS, and then there is the man with two children. Much of the pain LGBTQ persons suffer is pain of this kind.There is no cause for which legal action can give relief or social action can eliminate. This is the condition of our lives.

When our friends die and leave us bereft. When our friends leave us. When opportunity abandons us. When we do our best and that is not enough. When our government turns its most vicious, ignorant power on us. When the person who is supposed to offer us succor—our parent, our teacher, the priest, our friend—betrays us and judges us. This is a familiar theme in music, but not so much in literature. And yet, and yet. This is a novel about the moment in time when the pain experienced by the LGBTQ community is perhaps at its greatest and is the moment when least can be done about it. No one caused this. In 1991, there were no effective medications for AIDS. The national government under George H.W. Bush was indifferent and had none of the sense of urgency which it was displaying so ostentatiously in its determination to go to war with Iraq. It was the settled policy of the Bush Administration not to allow the federal government to provide any help or resources to any LGBTQ persons. The little group of friends around Alec Argento were not a group of perfect people, either. They all drank too much, and no one in *Winter Rain* mentions a self-help program like Alcoholics Anonymous or Al-Anon. Because of the conditions of their lives—they are not born into LGBTQ families—they have no or little communal knowledge, and they don't know what to ask of each other. They have almost no legal rights, and their communal rights are at the mercy of people who look on them mockingly or with a certain horror. The person who might have helped, like Alec's father, can't escape his bigotry, merely making things worse with his fly-by visits to Boston, his criticism, his ignorance of the basic conditions of his son's life, his self-satisfaction, and his constant mocking of his son. There are crimes committed in *Winter Rain* that go unnoticed or forgotten because their perpetrators are concentrating on larger matters or are too drunk to remember committing them. Alec pays heavily for his failure to be a decent father. But even at his worst, he instinctively does what he has to do for Amos. That is redeeming. Whether it is enough, I don't know. At the end, *Winter Rain* is close to an absolutely direct picture of a small community doing its thing during a period which rivals the plagues of Egypt. We want LGBTQ people to be virtuous when they fight back. But it is very clear that LGBTQ people fight back—and fight back clumsily but successfully—with the armies that they have, flawed as we are. LGBTQ literature, which includes *Winter Rain* and AIDS literature and the political literature of bigotry at this point in our history, is nearly identical to an epic war poem.

September 25, 2018

Earthrise 11

Conclusions

1

Neil Armstrong was difficult to live with and probably denied Janet, his wife, and his sons what they may have wanted most from him—warmth and love—but Armstrong stumbled into the one place on Earth where what was wanted from him was exactly what he had to offer—a man with an encyclopedic memory, a scientific orderliness to his mind unperturbed by emotion. If he had ever allowed the churning emotions inside to surface and to be revealed to other humans, he wouldn't be what he needed to be, which was an almost perfect person to command the first flight to the Moon.

The story of mankind's first flight to the Moon is a big story with a cast of thousands, but this is a smaller story than that. It is a story of Neil Armstrong's grieving his daughter's, Karen's, death from a brain tumor during his time in a test pilot program. It is unclear how he got into this program or how he got out. We are not shown how he achieved any of the other advances he made. We are shown one interview with a panel of senior men asking him questions, but his answers are minimal and bare. Neil moves from test pilot to astronaut-in-training to the Gemini program to the Apollo program to his final test as commander of the Apollo 11 mission to the Moon without ever having seemed to do anything to get himself there. He gets letters, people come to see him with news, and he is asked, "Will you do it?" and he answers, with a shrug, "Yes." Other astronauts are the ones to say, "Golly, gee, you want me? Sure, I'll do it." We never see him talk about his goals—what it is all about, this career of his—or what he wants from life.

Apparently, this story is the story of his grief for his child, and how, being the person he is, he can't express his grief and so can't get rid of it. Others try to help him with it—his wife, his fellow astronauts, his seniors at NASA—but he can't let go of it. It may be that a gesture he makes toward the end of the stay on the Moon is meant for us to understand as bringing closure, but it is so minimal that it is not clear, and we are left with the realization that Neil Armstrong probably carries this grief with him to the grave. Armstrong carries this grief against the background of the sixties, the Kennedy and Johnson and Nixon Administrations, and the Space Program which produced the Gemini and Apollo programs and finally the flight of Apollo 11 to the Moon, commanded by Neil Armstrong. There are what seem to be parties at the astronauts' houses, a cocktail party at the White House, Congressional investigations into accidents and deaths, and moments at which a spacecraft is spinning out of control. But a constant through all this is visual images of the Moon in what seem to be all its phases, floating beyond the trees at various points in the Armstrong's back yard in Houston, in some other astronaut's back yard, every nighttime scene, sometimes emphasized by being placed in the center of the screen, and sometimes off to the side. Scenes may end, and then the camera slides up until it captures the Moon. Then we know the scene has ended. These astronauts, the other actors, the director, the characters, all are obsessed with this celestial body. For more than NASA, more than all the business of being an astronaut, what dominates these images is the Moon itself, which is the point. And yet, Armstrong grieves.

It might be said that the narrative swaps off the values of home for the values of work—Neil Armstrong regularly seems to put his job before his family—but that is not so. The director takes both sides of the narrative and twists them so that it becomes impossible to separate them and to see Armstrong's personal, private story distinct from the immense, public story bigger than any other single story since World War II. Armstrong—the man he is—doesn't change. And yet, it feels like a tragedy to see him boxed up inside himself as we do, even while what he is doing is changing mankind's place in the cosmos, and we need him just this way.

The First Man, which has drawn me in twice to see it, is about the character of the epic hero. Neil Armstrong is the man needed to complete his epic tasks, but his character causes him to suffer, and the events that formed him are unalterable.

In *The First Man,* the director brings the two halves of the film together at the point, near the end, when Neil Armstrong is standing on the edge of a crater on the surface of the Moon. The audience cannot see Armstrong because he is entirely encased in his white space suit. He opens his hand. What the audience sees in the opening white glove encasing his hand is the small plastic bracelet of beads which we can see spells out K A R E N. It's the kind of bracelet that hospitals put on hospitalized children to identify them during their stay. Small, white, plastic, a little letter on each bead, which is cube-shaped. They used to be put on newborns. Slowly, Armstrong's gloved hand, which takes up the whole screen in an IMAX Cinema, opens and the small plastic bracelet slides out of his hand and falls slowly into the black shadow of the crater, falls so slowly that the white color that is the bracelet takes several seconds to disappear in the blackness. At that point, the two halves of the film come together—Armstrong's grief and the race to the Moon—and for many the race to the Moon is subsumed into Armstrong's attempt to deal with his grief.

But something else is going on. Early in the film, Neil Armstrong says, "When you get a different vantage point, it changes your perspective." What if you had some other one, some being arrive on the Moon from some other planet, and the only artifact he or she found was the small white beaded bracelet with the capital letters K A R E N on it? It makes of Armstrong's gesture an entirely different thing. Armstrong's gesture becomes an artifact of our civilization, and while it remains a marker of Armstrong's relationship with his daughter and more distantly with his civilization, it becomes also an artifact of an unknown civilization. A person finding the bracelet probably won't know the connection between the owner of the bracelet and where that person was from, but, like the Rosetta Stone, the bracelet will serve as an introduction to our alphabet, our system of denomination, our chemistry and to our language. It may be the beginning of his getting to know us. The plastic bracelet Neil Armstrong leaves in the crater on the Moon is a key to who we are.

2

Viewed from the perspective of *Earthrise*, the photograph brought back from space of the Earth, rising up in the distance beyond the Moon, the Moon itself in the foreground, with its implications of circularity, of rising and falling, of creation and destruction, of life in the empty blackness of space on our tiny beautiful blue marble, the pain in *Winter Rain*—pain and confusion and bewilderment—that I was writing about in the last posting, Earthrise 10, finds its home on that beautiful blue marble falling through space. As do *David*, and *The Brandenburg Concertos*, and a portrait of Maria Therese by Pablo Picasso. These paradoxes are implicit everywhere in our lives on this Earth, including the LGBTQ lives under consideration here.

There is a perhaps apocryphal story about Picasso, who is believed to have once said, "When I was a child my mother said to me, 'If you become a soldier, you will become a general. If you become a monk, then you will end up as Pope.' Instead, I became a painter, and wound up as Picasso." *https://www.pablopicasso.org*

Picasso wasn't talking about what his paintings are worth, although I think that is what his mother was talking about. And he wasn't talking about his fame, although I think she was probably talking about that too. She was probably talking about the fact that he was going to be a leader, become the most important, in any field he entered. We don't know from this snippet what else she thought of, aside from the military and the priesthood. There are men and women who go for power, but that seems counter-intuitive when applied to Picasso. What did he mean, when he said, *wound up as Picasso?* How does one get to be Picasso? Since a person would not get to be Picasso by setting out to be rich or powerful or holy or famous, he must have done it by painting.

The most famous *political* painting in the twentieth century is *Guernica,* which Picasso painted after the nationalists bombed the small Spanish town of Guernica in 1937. The painting depicts the anguish and anger the painter felt at the murder of the townspeople and animal life of Guernica, the chaos of aerial bombing, and the destruction and dismemberment of the animal life in the town of Guernica during the Spanish Civil War. Picasso deposited the painting at the Museum of Modern Art in Manhattan, to remain there until democracy was restored to Spain and the painting could be given to the Prado in Madrid. In the middle of all his other paintings, there is this painting.

3

My four books are political novels. This is the way I wrote my political novels. If I were to write about about a person's life, emphasizing the unity of it, I would need to deemphasize the chronology of it. As it happened, what I did was to start off with a brief mention of a wall in our host's condo in Provincetown, which held a thicket of framed snapshots of men on the beach, all beautiful, many naked, many of whom were now dead of AIDS or moved to Somerville, or Amherst, or who had become the director of some non-profit organization benefitting the LGBTQ community. This was followed by short descriptions of moments like snapshots from Fair Shaw's memory, beginning when he was three years old, of an intense homoerotic awareness, some even before he could have been aware of a homosexual attraction. Then there follows, for approximately one hundred pages, a sequence of episodes, in which Shaw becomes aware of corruptions in the images at the beginning—his family's obsession with their class, alcoholism, his own homosexuality, his family's conservative politics, their religion, during all of which Shaw seeks an answer to the question, which gradually takes on substance as different characters repeat the question in different ways and from different perspectives, *How can I be a homosexual and be respected?* Of course, in the end, Shaw learns he has to respect himself because the others don't matter.

This first part of *Race Point Light* establishes the way the book moves forward—a rough chronology setting forth a series of moments that are linked by theme. The idea behind the second part takes Shaw into the US Army, to college, to New York, to graduate school, to the Civil Rights movement, and is something like *How do I deal with it?* and ends with his proposal of marriage to a woman. In each of these parts, Shaw explores what the culture means by "homosexual"—it's a sickness, a sin, a crime, a source of great danger, a violation of his vows to his wife, the source of unimaginable hope, profound enlightenment, and pleasure—and tries out various ways of living with it. He tells various people—his brother, various soldiers, a fellow graduate student, a priest, the woman he is about to marry, various psychologists and psychiatrists— all of whom, it was apparent, knew less about the subject than he did. And, it was also clear, none of the adults around Shaw wanted to know about this subject what Shaw knew about it. As he said to himself about his mother when he was an adolescent, *She doesn't want to know what I know.*

There is a moment, in the middle of *Ceremonies*, when a man on a landing of a staircase at the local university, looking out the window at the students crossing campus between classes, says to Derek, *What do gays want?* Thereafter, the question reverberates through different episodes. It has earlier manifestations, when the Coalition meets the first time and members of the community are invited to come forward and say what they want the Coalition to focus on. Deborah, early in Part 3, suggests an answer, and Dana, in the final episode of the novel, stands in line to vote in the presidential election in November, 1984, a kind of ultimate choice, but she remembers back in June, before Bernie Mallett was murdered, walking in Gay Pride down Charles Street and hearing someone shout, "What do gays want?" and hearing the mass of marchers shout back, "Freedom!" "And when do we want it?" "Now!" But even though they weren't very clear about what freedom meant, they were clear about wanting it.

But they don't get it. They get murder and savage beatings. A reader spoke very movingly about *Ceremonies*—"It was the first gay novel," she said, "that addressed the lives of working class gay people."—but that was before she finished the book. Later, she told me, "I didn't know you were going to end the book that way." She had not liked my choices.

Of course, a novel, which proceeds through time, has to end at some point, and sometimes that point is the moment of a beating or a murder, a resolution of the stresses of the story. But there are other ways to end a story. Describing the same actions on the same dates, the writer could conclude the narrative with the events in this order: around Halloween in Boston, the School Board meeting, the 1984 election. In paintings, in the fourteenth century, the artist may place one part of the story in the foreground and another part of the story above. A viewer might see the School Board meeting on one side and the 1984 election above, and the events around Halloween in Boston on the other side, and the viewer would see them all at the same time. *Guernica* works this way. Time, before and after, has nothing to do with *Guernica*. This exists, and that exists, and they exist in the same moment. *The Wasteland* works this way.

4

Some sculptures, some poetry, also work this way. And it is a fine thought to know that pictorial art can function this way. I walk Commercial Street in Provincetown and pass the galleries. The paintings on the walls of AMP exist at the same time as paintings on the Bowersock gallery's walls. In my mind, they hang together.

The point here is that the graphite drawing of the man's beautiful body, lying stretched out across the canvas, exists in the same space as *Guernica*. The beautiful and the horrific. At The Globe theatre in London in 1601, watching *Twelfth Night* and *Hamlet* on the same stage, with the same actors, on the same day, it was inevitable that the playgoer would not feel jarred, would, in fact, think t*hat's the way my life is*. Once, a relative read something I had written, and said to me, "Next time, write something cheerful." I was pissed, but if that were to happen again, I would say, *Come back tomorrow. There's a new show.* Or *Check out the next shelf, where you'll find Satire.* Or *On Thursdays we do Comedy.* Or t*his afternoon, for a matinee. We have all the actors ready.*

But I don't know what will happen next time. There are no limits on the subject of novels about heterosexuals or for that matter about homosexuals. What limits there are which exist on the subject of any work of art are merely a matter of taste and therefore may be violated at the artist's choice and the gallery-visitor's inclination.

I was in London one year and was bemused by what seemed like the limited number of the professional actors we saw. At the Barbican, the actor playing Ariel could be seen playing some heavy part on the TV and some major tragic figure in the Workshop Theatre downstairs. One group of actors seem to be playing all the roles all over London. Helen Mirren seemed to be playing all of them.

On our Earth there are a limited number of us to play all the parts, and a limited number of parts to play of all that have been written. And yet, we seem to like to watch the same shows with the same actors over and over again, or, to change the art form, to read the same books and the same plots. I started writing too late in my life to have written many of these stories—I was 45 when I started—but there are many millions of stories to be written about LGBTQ persons and the same number about other kinds of persons. These are ours, here on Earth. I wanted to write about how painful it was living here, because the knowledge of what happened to us should not be lost. Someone had to write about Charles Howard's death. We owed him that. A gravestone in Provincetown says, *Nelson White, Lost at Sea*. LGBTQ persons live many different lives, both comic and tragic, and in one life, epic and lyric. A queer may experience both comedy and tragedy, and there is no need to choose between them. No possibility even.

Today is Sunday. On Thursday, the ashes of Matthew Shepard were interred in the Washington National Cathedral. Matthew Shepard was born on December 1, 1976, and died, tied to a fence near Laramie, Wyoming, on October 12, 1998, his ashes buried October 26, 2018, in the Washington National Cathedral. Charles Howard was murdered on July 7, 1984, in Bangor, Maine. He was beaten, stripped naked, and thrown off a bridge into a small river, where he drowned. These two young men, who died in different parts of the United States, fourteen years apart, in circumstances which were very similar, prompted a response from their towns which was very different. When Charles Howard died, his town largely turned its back on him. When Matthew Shepard died, the times had changed, and his community—and his nation—couldn't bear the image of the beautiful boy tied to the fence on the prairie, dying. Both young men have had novels written about their deaths.

So for the writer, it is not merely a question of choosing

between this subject and that. It becomes a question of what a writer needs to write. The answer is all of it. Every grain of sand. The challenge writers face is the plain difficulty of writing novels about vast areas of LGBTQ lives which have been totally ignored. We are only just getting to the point of defining transgender and have not written many stories in which a transgender person is at its center. We are still writing stories in which the LGBTQ person is coming out. It's a kind of fairy tale that Bruno Bettelheim analyzes, and we read it over and over for the reasons that Bettelheim puts forth. It is a deeply satisfying narrative for those not yet fully grown. This leaves, for an easy category of stories still to be written, the whole library of stories in which the LGBTQ person is dying. Or learning the cello. Or joining the rebels in whatever revolution they are in on whatever continent. This leaves a story about the gay person who succeeds in the difficult world of big business or who is an archeologist in Iraq in 1998 to be written next, to be given the full treatment of an intelligent, aware, sophisticated narrative in which her story can be told.

What our writers may consider themselves free to write about when they open their computers is the whole range of the human condition. Publishers are known to reject books that will not attract a broad sales. With LBGTQ books, they seek "cross-over books" which will raise their sales and make fat their bottom line. Even LGBTQ writers are frequently known to tell us all that publishing is not a charity and that it exists to make money for the publisher. Well, if we learn the value of books that are not from our community and if others learn the value of LGBTQ books, some of that problem will be solved. We could read each other's books. Ebooks and print-on-demand will solve other issues. But the first issue to which LGBTQ writers can address themselves is the question, *What*

important LGBTQ novels have not yet been written? and know
its corollary answer, *I will write that one.*

5

Writers, artists, whether they see us living in a comedy or a
tragedy—or some problem play—all seem to commit
themselves to an endeavor, to make something. To create
something. Sometimes the something is sad or tragic,
uncomfortable or ugly, and sometimes it is *Midsummer Night's
Dream*, surpassingly beautiful, or *Twelfth Night*. But what is
true is that *Lear* and *Midsummer Night's Dream* are both
surpassingly beautiful creations of our species. A performance
of either one exalts the playgoer. This is also true of George
Balanchine's choreography, Jackson Pollock's paintings,
Augustus Saint-Gaudens, Rodin, Picasso paintings and
sculptures, Lucien Freud's portraits, Marlon Brando's acting,
Helen Mirren, and Brad Pitt, and while you may weep at what
you see in the museum or theatre or cinema and thousands of
others, that same creation will make you proud or grateful to
have seen it. *What a great thing that was just now. I am lucky
to have seen that.*

 There is no limit to the subject of art, and depending on the
intent of the artist, *it will make you laugh or cry,* and our
literature—*the literature of people who make up the LGBTQ
communities*—will, eventually, encompass every single thing *in
our live*s.

6

If you were standing on the moon, you'd have a different

120

perspective. My husband and I saw *The First Man* last night and, figuratively, stood on the Moon and saw Earth falling through space in front of us—in front of us—Earth with its millions of stories. Earth, and the United States in particular, during the Twentieth Century, has had many victories that have brought us more freedom. Many of these are court judgments, in cases brought by people who considered this or that book to be "obscene." People wanted to prevent gay writers from writing about some of our subjects.

I won't bother to attempt to define obscenity here, but it is important to note the cases—rather like always remembering what *Brown v. Board of Education* was about and when it happened and what resulted from it. These obscenity cases are, for readers and for writers and taken together, our *Brown v. Board of Education*, a bedrock, unarguable statement of our right to write and to read what we wish, that our lives, in literary form, are protected by the Constitution. These cases are important because, for a long time, we were not allowed to write anything that could be considered "perverse" and the very suggestion of a homosexual relationship in a novel was enough to get the novel defined as "obscene" and therefore unpublishable and beyond the protection of the First Amendment. This is no longer the case, but the effects of the centuries of censorship of LGBTQ literature are still strong enough to call people who are not gay themselves to refuse to read books that they may have heard about, because they have heard about its subject.

In my life, the first documented case of governmental censorship of literature was of James Joyce's great novel, *Ulysses*, published in Paris by Sylvia Beach's Shakespeare & Co. and published in the US by Random House. The case is called *United States v. One Book Entitled "Ulysses,"* and the judge was a federal district judge named, wonderfully, Learned

Hand. The case was decided in 1933, twenty-four years before I graduated from high school, and when I bought my first copy, Random House had bound into my copy Judge Hand's decision liberating the book. It made a huge impression on me. It was my first novel by James Joyce, and it was my first legal decision by anybody. The book had been charged with being obscene. And whenever I wanted to I could read Judge Hand's decision saying it was not obscene. This decision was later affirmed by Judge John M. Woolsey of the 2nd Circuit. What came out of this censorship case was that the government had to look at the book as a whole and not merely at the writer's use of one obscene word. The Judge ruled: "Each word of the book contributes like a bit of mosaic to the detail of the picture which Joyce is seeking to construct for his readers." And that included the word *fuck*. And *suck*. After this one, cases were brought against *Lolita* and *Tropic of Cancer*, as well as many many others. Ultimately, all of these books were freed to be published. When *Faggots* was published, no one cared very much. That's where we want it to be.

While the right to read anything has been expanding over the whole of the United States, another movement has been going in the other direction during the last century. Courts are not supportive of the idea of banning books, and our Constitution gives them many ways to protect literature. But the anti-literature folks have found other means.

Gay and lesbian and bisexual and transgender and queer people have suffered through centuries in which they were neither allowed to write about their lives nor read about them. This is less of a problem now, but it is still a problem. The literary review of the school I originally went to, later published announcements inviting submissions of poems and short stories. The announcement said that *No story with a homosexual theme will be accepted*. The consequences of

centuries of censorship remain with us. Were some intelligent
creature to land on the Moon and find Karen's bracelet and
then be able to translate texts from the Library of Congress, for
example, in addition to centuries of literature about
heterosexual men and women living on Earth, now, in 2018,
they would find a mere sixty or eighty years of a literature
devoted to all the other kinds of people who don't think there
are only two genders or only one gender object choice, a
literature largely thinned out by censorship and self-censorship,
composed of stories about what it was like to be gay and to live
on Earth in 2018. The censorship is real and has had real
consequences.

    There are different kinds of censorship. Censorship may
operate through the publisher. Publishers, as they tell us over
and over, are in the business of making money, and they have a
complex formula by which they measure whether a book will
make money. Those that aren't predicted to make money are
rejected. On the other hand, a book that the publishers agree
will make money goes through the editing process a few times
and then is printed, perhaps, for a 100,000 copies. Another
publisher, not demanding as much at the bottom line as
publisher number 1, decides to publish ten books, each of
which has to be edited at least once before it is printed for
10,000 copies. Notice that publisher number 2 is offering the
reader a far greater variety of books than publisher number 1.
But a publisher, trying to decide whether to publish one book
and sell 100,000 copies or ten books and sell 10,000 each,
notes that the overhead for the one-book-at-100,000 copies is
one-tenth the size of the ten-books-at-10,000. Savings at scale.
And what gets left out is the minority like ours that doesn't
have 100,000 book purchasers to make our books financially
viable for either of the big publishers. What is the minority to
do that only has 5,000 members, of whom only 3,000 are

serious book readers? The only solution, for the publisher, is to buy only books that are crossover books—books that appeal to both gay and straight and therefore together make the sales necessary to keeping the publishing house in the black.

But a small minority like ours is out of luck if we can't get enough of our own to make the necessary purchases. If we write a book on a subject that many LGBTQ people want to read about—AIDS, for example, or marriage equality, or bigotry—and people who are knowledgeable about novels say that it is a very good book for LGBTQ people, and yet the publishers won't publish it—this is censorship-by-bottom line. The publisher uses his demand for a return on his investment— which is his right—as a reason for his refusal to publish your book. His or her refusal to serve a small minority is a kind of bigotry. And it is definitely a kind of censorship. The books that get published are attractive to the largest demographic in the country—white straight people—and contain nothing that will discomfit the sensibilities of the white straight people who may be enticed into reading a gay book, and don't contain a homophobic white man who is from a "good family" and with degrees from an Ivy League school. The large majority of our community is out of luck, at least as far as the big publishers are concerned. When I had completed my first novel— *Ceremonies*, about the events surrounding the murder of Charles Howard—I submitted the novel to a person who was said to be the biggest and best gay literary agent in New York. She had heard about my manuscript and asked to see it. She read it and said, "This is a wonderful novel." Then, without pausing for breath, she said, "But no publisher in New York will publish it." We discussed this for a while—my contributions to the discussion mainly focussed on the idea that I had thought that it was the job of agents to persuade publishers that they should publish "wonderful" books. Her contribution focussed on that fact that she didn't think it was a "cross-over" book. Other publishers complained that there were no straight characters "so you've only told half the story." I kept insisting that I didn't write my book for straight people or to appeal to straight people or to answer the needs of straight people. I had written my book for LGBTQ people, but they refused to publish it.

We actually have more options as LGBTQ writers and readers than we have ever had before. It could be said that we live in a golden age of publishing. On our computers on which we write our books, we can create ebooks on which readers who want to can read our books. An iPad Mini 4 is lighter (.65 lbs) than a printed *Race Point Light* (1.9 lbs in print) and uses less paper from forests, for those of us who are realizing that there is not an unending supply of trees on Earth. And, brand new to my awareness is print-on-demand, a technology that has been around for thirty years, but is just getting to the point of being available to an LGBTQ writer, at home in their workroom. A print-on-demand book, like the ebook, cuts out the big publishers entirely. It is a technology that allows you to buy a copy of a book, on line, and the company on the other end will print one copy for you, skipping the 10,000 copies that may usually be printed and shipped and stored and shipped and then distributed to bookstores around the country. Even print-on-demand is better for the planet than regular printing. If your book only attracts five buyers, then only five copies are printed, and the Earth is only short one tree rather than a forest. The big New York publishers have concealed from the reading public the fact that when a single reader wants to read a single book, he or she must join with 10,000 other people who are all predictably going to want that particular book. This is a system designed for people whose reading tastes are similar to those of a large crowd.

Two final points here: Adriana Books, which publishes *Ceremonies, Race Point Light, Winter Rain,* and *Adam in the Morning,* in both ebook and print-on-demand forms, and many other similar publishers, free the writer from the chokehold the big publishers have had on what we can read and what we can get our friends to read, and correct the error that has developed in the publishing industries that is bad for the Earth—that is, paper books and their massive use of the earth's resources. The effect of these two changes, which are linked together, is to make our books more interesting, more diverse, and cheaper and kinder to the Earth. Now there is a greater chance that the record of our lives in fiction, freed of the control of the giant publishers, will be more complete than it has been in the past, and will include the private grief of LGBTQ people like Alec Argento and Fair Shaw and the little group who knew Charles Howard and described with the same care in our novels as *The First Man* describes Neil Armstrong's grief for Karen and as *The Tree of Life* describes Mrs. O'Brien's grief for her son. I write for a press free of the constraints that gay books—all but those by the most powerful voices—have always experienced. Big bookstores have reduced the space they devote to us down to one shelf. This series, the *Earthrise* essays, and the four novels to which they refer, have been my frank attempt to fight back.

November 25, 2019

Sources

Bruno Bettelheim. *The Uses of Enchantment: The Meaning and Importance of Fairy Tales*. New York: Alfred A. Knopf, 1976.

David Carter, *Stonewall: The Riots that Sparked the Gay Revolution*. New York: St Martin's Press, 2004

Dwight Cathcart. *Ceremonies*. Boston: Adriana Books, 2002.

_____. *Adam in the Morning*. Boston: Adriana Books, 2010.

_____. *Race Point Light*. Boston: Adriana Books, 2005.

_____. *Winter Rain*. Boston: Adriana Books, 2018.

Damien Chazelle, Director. *The First Man*. Ryan Gosling, Claire Foy, released October 12, 2018

John Donne. *The Complete English Poems, ed.* A. J. Smith. New York: Penguin Books, 1971.

Daniel D'Addario. "The Straight Canon is Very Gay." http://www.salon.com/the-straight-canon-is-very-gay.

Daniel D'Addario. "Where's the Buzzed-About Gay Novel." http://www.salon.com/2013/07/31/wheres_the_buzzed_about_gay_novel?

.

Sources

Martin Duberman. *Stonewall*. New York: A Dutton Book.1993/

Jaime Harker. *Middlebrow Queer: Christopher Isherwood in America*. Minneapolis: University of Minnesota Press, 2013.

Dylan Jones. *Attitude*. "Young queer people shouldn't be obliged to care about LGBT history." https://attitude.co.uk/ article/young-queer-people-shouldnt-be-obliged-to-care-about-lgbt-history-and-thats-the-biggest-sign-of-success-there-is-opinion-1/17046/

Alfred Kinsey, Wardell Pomeroy, Clyde Martin. *Sexual Behavior in the Human Male*. Philadelphia: W. B. Saunders Company, 1949.

Terence Malick, Director, *Tree of Life*, starring Brad Pitt, Sean Penn, Cottonwood Pictures, 2011.

Herman Melville, *Moby Dick*. Penguin Books, 1992.

Christopher Potter, *The Earth Gazers: On seeing Ourselves*. New York. Pegasus Books, 2018

Lance Richardson. *Slate:* "Family Jewels."https://slate.com/ human-interest/2018/05/queer-history-matters-because-it-offers-tradition-and-belonging.html May 4, 2018.

Frances Stoner Saunders, *The Cultural Cold War: The CIA in the World of Arts and Letters*. New York: New Press, 2001.

William Shakespeare. *King Lear*. New York: A Signet Classic, A New American Library, 1963.

Sources

Keith Spencer. "How seeing earth from space changes you," *Salon*, March 3, 2018

George Will. "Has the Catholic Church committed the worse crime in US history?" *Washington Post.* https://www.washingtonpost.com/opinions/has-the-catholic-church-committed-the-worst-crime-in-us-history/2019/03/12/1875bb84-44ee-11e9-8aab-95b8d80a1e4f_story.html.

Somerville, Massachusetts
2019

www.ingramcontent.com/pod-product-compliance
Lightning Source LLC
Chambersburg PA
CBHW031519270326
41930CB00006B/434